AAT

Qualification ~~and Credit~~ Framework (QCF)
AQ2013
LEVEL 3 DIPLOMA IN ACCOUNTING
(QCF)

QUESTION BANK

Accounts Preparation

2015 Edition

College of North West London
Willesden Learning Resources Centre
Dudden Hill Lane NW10 2XD

For assessments from September 2015

633305
KT-416-532

633305   657.076: ACCOUNTING

Third edition June 2015
ISBN 9781 4727 2200 3

Previous edition
ISBN 9781 4727 0934 9

British Library Cataloguing-in-Publication Data
A catalogue record for this book is available from the British
Library

Published by
BPP Learning Media Ltd
BPP House
Aldine Place
London W12 8AA

www.bpp.com/learningmedia

Printed in the United Kingdom by Martins of Berwick
Sea View Works
Spittal
Berwick-Upon-Tweed
TD15 1RS

Your learning materials, published by BPP Learning Media Ltd,
are printed on paper obtained from traceable sustainable
sources.

All our rights reserved. No part of this publication may be
reproduced, stored in a retrieval system or transmitted, in any
form or by any means, electronic, mechanical, photocopying,
recording or otherwise, without the prior written permission of
BPP Learning Media Ltd.

The contents of this book are intended as a guide and not for
professional advice. Although every effort has been made to
ensure that the contents of this book are correct at the time of
going to press, BPP Learning Media makes no warranty that
the information in this book is accurate or complete and accept
no liability for any loss or damaged suffered by any person
acting or refraining from acting as a result of the material in this
book.

We are grateful to the AAT for permission to reproduce the
AAT sample assessment(s). The answers to the AAT sample
assessment(s) have been published by the AAT. All other
answers have been prepared by BPP Learning Media Ltd.

©
BPP Learning Media Ltd
2015

CONTENTS

Introduction   v

Question and answer bank

Chapter tasks	Questions	Answers
1 Accounting principles	3	71
2 Accounting concepts	8	76
3 Purchase of non-current assets	10	77
4 Depreciation of non-current assets	15	82
5 Disposal of non-current assets	19	86
6 Accruals and prepayments	22	89
7 Inventory	25	92
8 Irrecoverable debts and doubtful debts	28	95
9 Bank reconciliations	32	98
10 Control account reconciliations	37	101
11 The trial balance, errors and the suspense account	43	105
12 The extended trial balance	53	111
AAT AQ2013 Sample Assessment 1	123	139
AAT AQ2013 Sample Assessment 2	149	165
BPP Practice Assessment 1	175	187
BPP Practice Assessment 2	195	207
BPP Practice Assessment 3	217	229
BPP Practice Assessment 4	237	249

A NOTE ABOUT COPYRIGHT

Dear Customer

What does the little © mean and why does it matter?

Your market-leading BPP books, course materials and e-learning materials do not write and update themselves. People write them on their own behalf or as employees of an organisation that invests in this activity. Copyright law protects their livelihoods. It does so by creating rights over the use of the content.

Breach of copyright is a form of theft – as well being a criminal offence in some jurisdictions, it is potentially a serious breach of professional ethics.

With current technology, things might seem a bit hazy but, basically, without the express permission of BPP Learning Media:

- Photocopying our materials is a breach of copyright

- Scanning, ripcasting or conversion of our digital materials into different file formats, uploading them to facebook or emailing them to your friends is a breach of copyright

You can, of course, sell your books, in the form in which you have bought them – once you have finished with them. (Is this fair to your fellow students? We update for a reason). Please note the e-products are sold on a single user licence basis: we do not supply 'unlock' codes to people who have bought them secondhand.

And what about outside the UK? BPP Learning Media strives to make our materials available at prices students can afford by local printing arrangements, pricing policies and partnerships which are clearly listed on our website. A tiny minority ignore this and indulge in criminal activity by illegally photocopying our material or supporting organisations that do. If they act illegally and unethically in one area, can you really trust them?

INTRODUCTION

This is BPP Learning Media's AAT Question Bank for Accounts Preparation. It is part of a suite of ground-breaking resources produced by BPP Learning Media for the AAT's assessments under the Qualification and Credit Framework.

The Accounts Preparation assessment will be **computer assessed**. As well as being available in the traditional paper format, this **Question Bank is available in an online environment** containing tasks similar to those you will encounter in the AAT's testing environment. BPP Learning Media believe that the best way to practise for an online assessment is in an online environment. However, if you are unable to practise in the online environment you will find that all tasks in the paper Question Bank have been written in a style that is as close as possible to the style that you will be presented with in your online assessment.

This Question Bank has been written in conjunction with the BPP Text, and has been carefully designed to enable students to practise all of the learning outcomes and assessment criteria for the units that make up Accounts Preparation. It is fully up to date as at June 2015 and reflects both the AAT's unit guide and the sample assessment(s) provided by the AAT.

This Question Bank contains these key features:

- Tasks corresponding to each chapter of the Text. Some tasks are designed for learning purposes, others are of assessment standard

- AAT's AQ2013 sample assessments and answers for Accounts Preparation and further BPP practice assessments

The emphasis in all tasks and assessments is on the practical application of the skills acquired.

VAT

You may find tasks throughout this Question Bank that need you to calculate or be aware of a rate of VAT. This is stated at 20% in these examples and questions.

Approaching the assessment

When you sit the assessment it is very important that you follow the on screen instructions. This means you need to carefully read the instructions, both on the introduction screens and during specific tasks.

When you access the assessment you should be presented with an introductory screen with information similar to that shown below (taken from the introductory screen from the AAT's AQ2013 Sample Assessment for Accounts Preparation).

We have provided the following assessment to help you familiarise yourself with AAT's e-assessment environment. It is designed to demonstrate as many as possible of the question types you may find in a live assessment. It is not designed to be used on its own to determine whether you are ready for a live assessment.

Each task is independent. You will not need to refer to your answers to previous tasks.
Read every task carefully to make sure you understand what is required.

Where the date is relevant, it is given in the task data.

Both minus signs and brackets can be used to indicate negative numbers UNLESS task instructions say otherwise.

The standard rate of VAT is 20%.

You must use a full stop to indicate a decimal point.
For example, write 100.57 NOT 100,57 or 100 57

You may use a comma to indicate a number in the thousands, but you don't have to.
For example, 10000 and 10,000 are both OK.

Other indicators are not compatible with the computer-marked system.

Complete all 6 tasks.

The actual instructions will vary depending on the subject you are studying for. It is very important you read the instructions on the introductory screen and apply them in the assessment. You don't want to lose marks when you know the correct answer just because you have not entered it in the right format.

In general, the rules set out in the AAT Sample Assessment for the subject you are studying for will apply in the real assessment, but you should again read the information on this screen in the real assessment carefully just to make sure. This screen may also confirm the VAT rate used if applicable.

A full stop is needed to indicate a decimal point. We would recommend using minus signs to indicate negative numbers and leaving out the comma signs to indicate thousands, as this results in a lower number of key strokes and less margin for error when working under time pressure. Having said that, you can use whatever is easiest for you as long as you operate within the rules set out for your particular assessment.

You have to show competence throughout the assessment and you should therefore complete all of the tasks. Don't leave questions unanswered.

In some assessments written or complex tasks may be human marked. In this case you are given a blank space or table to enter your answer into. You are told in the assessment which tasks these are (note: there may be none if all answers are marked by the computer).

If these involve calculations, it is a good idea to decide in advance how you are going to lay out your answers to such tasks by practising answering them on a word document, and certainly you should try all such tasks in this question bank and in the AAT's environment using the sample/practice assessments.

When asked to fill in tables, or gaps, never leave any blank even if you are unsure of the answer. Fill in your best estimate.

Note that for some assessments where there is a lot of scenario information or tables of data provided (eg tax tables), you may need to access these via 'pop-ups'. Instructions will be provided on how you can bring up the necessary data during the assessment.

Finally, take note of any task specific instructions once you are in the assessment. For example you may be asked to enter a date in a certain format or to enter a number to a certain number of decimal places.

Remember you can practise the BPP questions in this question bank in an online environment on our dedicated AAT Online page. On the same page is a link to the current AAT Sample Assessment as well.

If you have any comments about this book, please email nisarahmed@bpp.com or write to Nisar Ahmed, AAT Head of Programme, BPP Learning Media Ltd, BPP House, Aldine Place, London W12 8AA.

Question bank

Chapter 1 – Accounting principles

Task 1.1

Compete the sentences below by selecting the appropriate option from the Picklist.

The sales returns day book lists…	*2*	▼
The purchases day book lists…	*3*	▼
The purchases returns day book lists…	*4*	▼
The sales day book lists…	*1*	▼

Picklist:

invoices sent to customers
credit notes sent to customers
invoices received from suppliers
credit notes received from suppliers

Task 1.2

What are the two effects of each of these transactions for accounting purposes?

Transaction	Account 1			Account 2		
	Name	Increase ✓	Decrease ✓	Name	Increase ✓	Decrease ✓
Payment of £15,000 into a business bank account by an individual in order to start up a business						
Payment by cheque of £2,000 for rent of a business property						
Payment by cheque of £6,200 for purchase of a delivery van						
Payment by cheque of £150 for vehicle licence for the van						
Payment by cheque of £2,100 for goods for resale						

BPP
LEARNING MEDIA

Transaction	Account 1			Account 2		
	Name	Increase ✓	Decrease ✓	Name	Increase ✓	Decrease ✓
Sale of goods for cash and cheques of £870						
Purchase of goods for resale on credit for £2,800						
Payment by cheque for petrol of £80						
Sale of goods on credit for £3,400						
Payment by cheque of £1,500 to credit suppliers						
Payment by cheque of electricity bill of £140						
Receipt of cheque from credit customer of £1,600						
Withdrawal of £500 of cash for the owner's personal living costs						
Payment by cheque for petrol of £70						

Task 1.3

For each of the transactions in the previous activity enter the amounts into the ledger accounts given below, then balance each of the accounts and prepare a trial balance at the end of this initial period of trading.

Capital account

	£		£

BPP LEARNING MEDIA

Bank account

	£		£

Rent account

	£		£

Van account

	£		£

Van expenses account

	£		£

Purchases account

	£		£

Sales account

	£		£

Purchases ledger control account

	£		£

Sales ledger control account

	£		£

Electricity account

	£		£

Drawings account

	£		£

BPP
LEARNING MEDIA

Trial balance	Debit £	Credit £
Capital		
Bank		
Rent		
Van		
Van expenses		
Purchases		
Sales		
Payables ie purchases ledger control account		
Receivables ie sales ledger control account		
Electricity		
Drawings		

Task 1.4

A credit balance on a ledger account indicates

✓	
	An asset or an expense
	A liability or an expense
	An amount owing to the organisation
	A liability or a revenue item

Chapter 2 – Accounting concepts

Task 2.1

For each of the following statements determine which accounting principle or concept is being invoked:

(a) Computer software, although for long-term use in the business, is charged to the statement of profit or loss when purchased as its value is small in comparison to the hardware.

Principle/concept	

(b) The non-current assets of the business are valued at their carrying amount rather than the value for which they might be sold.

Principle/concept	

(c) The expenses that the business incurs during the year are charged as expenses in the statement of profit or loss even if the amount of the expense has not yet been paid in cash.

Principle/concept	

Task 2.2

The two fundamental qualitative characteristics of financial information, according to the IASB's *Conceptual Framework* are:

	and	

Task 2.3

Classify the following items as long-term assets ('non-current assets'), short-term assets ('current assets') or liabilities.

	Non-current assets ✓	Current assets ✓	Liabilities ✓
A PC used in the accounts department of a retail store			
A PC on sale in an office equipment shop			
Wages due to be paid to staff at the end of the week			
A van for sale in a motor dealer's showroom			
A delivery van used in a grocer's business			
An amount owing to a bank for a loan for the acquisition of a van, to be repaid over 9 months			

Chapter 3 – Purchase of non-current assets

Task 3.1

In each of the following circumstances determine how much capital expenditure has been incurred and how much revenue expenditure has been incurred by a business that is registered for VAT:

	Capital expenditure £	Revenue expenditure £
An SN63 sanding machine has been purchased at a cost of £12,000 plus VAT. The delivery charge was £400. After its initial run it was cleaned at a cost of £100.		
A building has been purchased at a cost of £120,000. The surveyor's fees were an additional £400 and the legal fees £1,200. The building has been re-decorated at a total cost of £13,000. Ignore VAT.		
A new main server has been purchased at a cost of £10,600. In order to house the server a room in the building has had to have a special air conditioning unit fitted at a cost of £2,450. The server's cost includes software worth £1,000 and CDs with a value of £100. Ignore VAT.		
A salesperson's car has been purchased at a cost of £14,000 plus VAT. The invoice also shows delivery costs of £50 (plus VAT) and road fund licence of £160 (no VAT charged). The car is not available for private use by the salesperson.		

Task 3.2

A business has just spent money on two of its machines. The SPK100 has been repaired after a breakdown at a cost of £2,400. The FL11 has had a new engine fitted at a cost of £3,100 which it is anticipated will extend its useful life to the business by four years.

The SPK100 repairs would be treated as:

✓	
	capital expenditure
	revenue expenditure

BPP LEARNING MEDIA

The FL11 repairs would be treated as:

	✓	
	capital expenditure	
	revenue expenditure	

Task 3.3

Draft journal entries for each of the following transactions by a business that is registered for VAT:

(a) Purchase of a salesperson's car for £12,000 plus VAT and road fund licence of £150 paid for by cheques. The car is not available for private use.

	Debit £	Credit £
Motor vehicles account		
VAT account		
Motor expenses account		
Bank account		

(b) Purchase of a machine for £15,400 plus VAT, on credit, and the alterations to the factory floor required that used employees' labour with a wage cost of £1,400.

	Debit £	Credit £
Machinery account		
VAT account		
Purchases ledger control account		
Wages account		

(c) Purchase of a computer for £3,800 plus VAT by cheque which included £100 of printer paper and £50 of CDs.

	Debit £	Credit £
Computer account		
Computer expenses account		
VAT account		
Bank account		

(d) Redecorating of the room which houses the computer prior to its installation, £800 paid by cheque. Ignore VAT.

	Debit £	Credit £
Building maintenance account		
Bank account		

(e) Insurance of the new computer was paid by cheque of £200. Ignore VAT.

	Debit £	Credit £
Computer expenses account		
Bank account		

Task 3.4

Write up the following transactions for a VAT registered business in the ledger accounts given:

(a) A machine was purchased for £13,500 plus VAT by cheque and installed using the business's own employees at a wage cost of £400 and own materials at a cost of £850.

(b) A building was purchased for £150,000 plus £20,000 of alterations in order to make it of use to the business. The unaltered parts of the building were then redecorated at a cost of £4,000. All purchases were paid for by cheque. Ignore VAT.

Machinery account

	£		£
Balance b/d	103,400.00		

Buildings account

	£		£
Balance b/d	200,000.00		

VAT account

	£		£
		Balance b/d	13,289.60

BPP
LEARNING MEDIA

Purchases account

	£		£
Balance b/d	56,789.50		

Wages account

	£		£
Balance b/d	113,265.88		

Buildings maintenance account

	£		£
Balance b/d	10,357.00		

Bank account

	£		£
Balance b/d	214,193.60		

Task 3.5

When a business uses its own work force to install some non-current assets, the cost of the labour may be added to the cost of the non-current asset.

	True
	False

Task 3.6

Which of the following costs would be classified as capital expenditure for a restaurant business?

✓	
	A replacement for a broken window
	Repainting the restaurant
	An illuminated sign advertising the business name
	Knives and forks for the restaurant

Task 3.7

Which of the following best explains what is meant by 'capital expenditure'?

Capital expenditure is expenditure:

✓	
	On non-current assets, including repairs and maintenance
	On expensive assets
	Relating to the acquisition or improvement of non-current assets
	Incurred by the chief officer of the business

BPP
LEARNING MEDIA

Chapter 4 – Depreciation of non-current assets

Task 4.1

The accounting concept that underlies the charging of depreciation is:

```
┌──────────────────────────────────────────────────┐
│                                                  │
└──────────────────────────────────────────────────┘
```

Task 4.2

Calculate the depreciation charge using the straight line method for each of the following non-current assets for the year ended 31 December 20X8. Also calculate the carrying amount of each asset at 31 December 20X8:

	Workings	Depreciation charge £	Carrying amount £
Machine purchased for £17,400 on 1 January 20X6 with a useful life of 5 years and a zero residual value.	17400 / 5	3480	
Machine purchased for £12,800 on 1 January 20X7 with a useful life of 4 years and a residual value of £2,000.		2700	
Computer purchased for £4,600 on 1 January 20X8 with a useful life of 3 years and an estimated resale value of £700.		1300	3300

Task 4.3

For each of the following non-current assets calculate the depreciation charge for the year ended 31 March 20X9 and the carrying amount at 31 March 20X9:

	Workings	Depreciation charge £	Carrying amount £
Machinery costing £24,600 purchased on 1 April 20X8 which is to be depreciated at 20% on the diminishing balance basis.		4920	19680
Motor vehicle costing £18,700 purchased on 1 April 20X6 which is to be depreciated at 20% on the diminishing balance basis.	?	9126	9574
Computer costing £3,800 purchased on 1 April 20X7 which is to be depreciated at 30% on the diminishing balance basis.	?	1938	1862

Task 4.4

Calculate the depreciation charge for the year ended 31 December 20X8 for each of the following non-current assets:

	Workings	Depreciation charge £
Machine purchased on 1 May 20X8 for £14,000. This is to be depreciated at the rate of 20% per annum on the straight-line basis. Depreciation is calculated on an annual basis and charged in equal instalments for each full month an asset is owned in the year.		1867
Office furniture and fittings purchased on 1 June 20X8 for £3,200. These are to be depreciated on the diminishing balance basis at a rate of 25% with a full year's charge in the year of purchase and no charge in the year of disposal.		800
Computer purchased on 31 October 20X8 for £4,400. This is to be depreciated at the rate of 40% per annum on the straight-line basis. Depreciation is calculated on an annual basis and charged in equal instalments for each full month an asset is owned in the year.		293

BPP LEARNING MEDIA

Task 4.5

On 1 January 20X0 a business purchased a laser printer costing £1,800. What are the annual depreciation charges for the accounting years ended 31 December 20X0, 20X1, 20X2 and 20X3 on the laser printer if the diminishing balance method is used at 60% per annum?

Note. Your workings should be to the nearest £.

1800

	Workings	Depreciation charge £
20X0		*1080*
20X1		*432*
20X2		*172.80*
20X3		*64.12*

1754

Task 4.6

What is the double entry for a depreciation charge for the accounting period?

Debit	✓
Credit	

Task 4.7

2437

July14 December14 1120
Jan15 572
" Jan16 - Dec16 46320
17 241.92

A machine was purchased for £2,800 on 1 July 20X4. The depreciation policy is to depreciate machinery on a diminishing balance basis at 40% per annum with a full year's charge in the year of purchase and no charge in the year of disposal. The business year end is 31 December.

What is the carrying amount of the machine at 31 December 20X7 (round to the nearest £)?

	£605
✓	£363
	£179
	£72

Task 4.8

What is the purpose of accounting for depreciation in financial statements?

✓	
✓	To allocate the cost less residual value of a non-current asset over the accounting periods expected to benefit from its use
	To ensure that funds are available for the eventual replacement of the asset
	To reduce the cost of the asset to its estimated market value
	To recognise the fact that assets lose their value over time

Chapter 5 – Disposal of non-current assets

Task 5.1

A non-current asset was purchased on 1 April 20X7 for £12,500 and is being depreciated at 30% per annum on the diminishing balance basis, with a full year's charge in the year of disposal. On 31 March 20X9 the asset was sold for £6,000.

What is the profit or loss on the sale of the non-current asset?

profit/loss	of £	

Task 5.2

A non-current asset was purchased on 1 January 20X6 for £25,000. It is being depreciated over its useful life of 5 years on the straight-line basis with a residual value of £3,000 and a full year's charge in the year of disposal. The asset was sold on 31 December 20X8 for £11,000.

Show the accounting entries for this asset from the day of purchase to the day of sale in the following ledger accounts. The business has a statement of financial position date of 31 December each year.

Non-current asset at cost account

	£		£
Bank	25000	Bal c/d	25000

Depreciation account

	£		£
Accumulated dep	4400	SPL	4400

Accumulated depreciation account

	£		£
Bal c/d	4400	Dep charge	4400
	4400		4400

Disposal account

	£		£
Vehicle at cost	25000	Accumulated dep	4400
		Bank	11000
		SPL	9600
	25000		25000

....

1 April 17 - 31 March 18   4140
1 April 18 - 31 March 19   2898
                          7038

Task 5.3

A motor vehicle had been purchased on 1 April 20X7 for £13,800 and has been depreciated on the diminishing balance basis at a rate of 30% per annum. It was sold on 31 March 20X9 for £7,000.

You are required to write up the ledger accounts for the year ended 31 March 20X9 to reflect the ownership and sale of this motor vehicle. A full year's charge for depreciation is to be charged in the year of disposal.

Depreciation expense account

	£		£
Accumulated dep	7038	SPL	7038

Accumulated depreciation account

	£		£
Bal c/d	7038	Dep charge	7038
	7038		7038

Motor vehicle at cost account

	£		£
Bank	13800	Bal c/d	13800
	13800		13800

Disposal account

	£		£
Vehicle at cost	13800	Accumulated	7038
SPL	238	Bank	7000

....

I Juy - 31Dec 16 => 1950   ?
I Jan 17 - 31Dec 17 => 3900
I Jan 18 - 30 Nov 18 => 3575
9425

Task 5.4

A machine was purchased on 30 June 20X6 for £15,600. The depreciation policy is to depreciate this asset at a rate of 25% per annum on a straight line basis. Depreciation is calculated on an annual basis and charged in equal instalments for each full month an asset is owned in the year. On 30 November 20X8 the machine was sold for £6,000. The business has an accounting year ending 31 December.

Write up the disposal account to reflect the disposal of this asset.

Disposal account

	£		£
machine at cost	15600	Accumulated dep	9425
		Bank	6000
		SPL - (loss)	175

Task 5.5

Your firm bought a machine for £5,000 on 1 January 20X1, which had an expected useful life of four years and an expected residual value of £1,000. Depreciation is on a straight line basis. On 31 December 20X3 the machine was sold for £1,600.

The amount to be entered in the 20X3 statement of profit or loss on disposal is:

✓	
	Profit of £600
	Loss of £600
	Profit of £350
✓	Loss of £400

I Jan - 31 Dec 11   1000
I Jan - 31 Dec 12   1000
I Jan - 31 Dec 13   1000
                    ____
                    3000

5000 | 3000
     | 1600
     ____
     SPL 400
        Loss

Chapter 6 – Accruals and prepayments

Task 6.1

During the year ended 31 March a business has paid £845 of telephone bills. However the bill for February and March has not been received and is expected to be approximately £170.

You are required to write up the following ledger account to reflect the telephone expense for the year showing the charge to the statement of profit or loss for the year.

Telephone account

	£		£
Bank	845	SPL	1015
Bal c/d	170		
	1015		1015

Task 6.2

Given below is the electricity expense account for the year ended 30 June for a business. At 30 June it is estimated from meter readings that the electricity bill for the final three months of the accounting year will be £900. The bill for £900 is eventually received and paid on 21 July.

You are required to write up the following ledger account showing the year end accrual and the charge to the statement of profit or loss for the year.

Electricity account

	£		£
30 June Bank	2,300	SPL	3200
Bal c/d	900		
	3200		3200

Task 6.3

The cash payments book for a business shows that in the year ended 31 May 20X8 £2,300 was paid for insurance. However this includes £250 for the year ending 31 May 20X9.

You are required to write up the insurance account to reflect this and to show the charge to the statement of profit or loss for the year.

Insurance account

	£		£
31 May Bank	2,300	Bal C/d	250
		SPL	2050
	2300		2300

BPP
LEARNING MEDIA

Task 6.4

A business pays rent for its premises in advance. The rent expense account for the year ending 30 June is given below but of this expense £400 is for the month of July.

You are required to write up the rent account to reflect this and to show the statement of profit or loss charge for the year.

Rent account

	£			£
30 June Bank	4,500	Bal C/d		400
		SPL		4100
	4500			4500

Task 6.5

A business sublets some of its premises to tenants who pay in advance. The rental income account for the year to 30 June is given below. £5,600 is received during the year of which £350 is in advance for the following month.

You are required to show the entries required in the rental income ledger account including the statement of profit or loss income figure for the year to 30 June.

Rental income account

	£	Bank		£
Bal c/d	350			5600
SPL	5250			
	5600			5600

Task 6.6   375

An electricity accrual of £375 was treated as a prepayment in preparing a business's statement of profit or loss for the year ended 31 December 20X4.

What was the resulting effect on the electricity expense of the business for the year?

	Overstated by £375
	Overstated by £750
	Understated by £375
✓	Understated by £750

Task 6.7

Cleverley Ltd started in business on 1 January 20X0, preparing accounts to 31 December 20X0. The electricity bills received were as follows.

		£
30 April 20X0	For 4 months to 30 April 20X0	5,279.47
31 July 20X0	For 3 months to 31 July 20X0	4,663.80
31 October 20X0	For 3 months to 31 October 20X0	4,117.28
31 January 20X1	For 3 months to 31 January 20X1	6,491.52

What should the electricity charge be for the year ended 31 December 20X0?

£ 18388.23

Task 6.8

At 31 December 20X0 the accounts of a business show accrued rent payable of £250. During 20X1 the business pays rent bills totalling £1,275, including one bill for £375 in respect of the quarter ending 31 January 20X2.

What is the statement of profit or loss charge for rent payable for the year ended 31 December 20X1?

£ 900

Task 6.9

During the year £5,000 rent was received. At the beginning of the year the tenant owed £1,000 and at the end of the year the tenant owed £500.

What was the rent received figure in the year's statement of profit or loss?

✓	
	£4,000
✓	£4,500
	£5,000
	£5,500

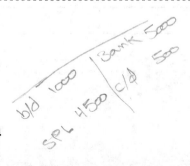

BPP LEARNING MEDIA

Chapter 7 – Inventory

Task 7.1

A business has 125 units of a product in inventory which cost £24.60 per unit plus £0.50 per unit of delivery costs. These goods can be sold for £25.80 per unit although in order to do this selling costs of £1.00 per unit must be incurred.

What is the cost of these units?

£ | 24.60 + 0.50

30.75
62.50
313.50
3137.50

What is their net realisable value?

£ | 25.80 - 1 = 24.80

At what value will the 125 units of the product be included in the extended trial balance?

£ | 24.60×125 = 3075

Task 7.2

A business has five lines of inventory. You are required to complete the table showing the value per unit for each line of the inventory and the total value to appear in the financial statements for this inventory.

Inventory line	Quantity – units	Cost £	Selling price £	Selling costs £	Value per unit £	Total value £
A	180	12.50	20.40	0.50		
B	240	10.90	12.60	1.80		
C	300	15.40	22.70	1.20		
D	80	16.50	17.80	1.50		
E	130	10.60	18.00	1.00		____
						____

IAS 2 lowest of Cost (or) NRV?

NRV = selling price – selling cost

Task 7.3

Given below are the movements on a line of inventory for the month of March:

1 Mar	Opening balance	80 units @ £8.20 656
7 Mar	Purchases	100 units @ £8.50 850
10 Mar	Sales	140 units
15 Mar	Purchases	180 units @ £8.70
26 Mar	Sales	100 units
31 Mar	Sales	70 units

What is the value of the closing inventory at 31 March using?

		£
(a)	the FIFO method	
(b)	the AVCO method	

unit

Total
656
850
1506

Task 7.4

Purchase 850

The rule for inventory is that it should be valued at:

Sale 140

£ lower cost and realisable value

80 × 8.20

Task 7.5

Dean Ltd's inventory includes three items for which the following details are available.

		Supplier's list price £	Net realisable value £
Product A		*36 37 8* 3,600	5,100
Product B	*G*	*277 9* 2,900	2,800
Product C		*903 10* 4,200	4,100
		10,700	12,000

The business receives a 2½% trade discount from its suppliers and it also takes advantage of a 2% discount for prompt payment.

What is the value of inventory to be shown in the statement of financial position?

£

BPP LEARNING MEDIA

Task 7.6

In relation to inventory, net realisable value means?

✓	
	The expected selling price of the inventory
✓	The expected selling price less disposal costs
	The replacement cost of the inventory
	The market price

Chapter 8 – Irrecoverable debts and doubtful debts

Task 8.1

A business which is not registered for VAT has receivables at the year end of £5,479. Of these it has been decided that £321 from G Simms & Co will never be received as this business has now gone into liquidation. A further debt for £124 from L Fitzgerald is also viewed as irrecoverable as L Fitzgerald cannot be traced and the debt is now 8 months overdue.

You are required to write off these irrecoverable debts in the general and sales ledger accounts given below showing any charge to the statement of profit or loss and the amended year end balances.

General ledger

Sales ledger control account

	£		£
Balance b/d	5,479	Irrecoverable debt	445
		Bal c/d	5034

Irrecoverable debts expense account

	£		£
SLCA	445	SPL	445

Sales ledger

G Simms & Co

	£		£
Bal b/d	321	Irrecoverable	321

L Fitzgerald

	£		£
Bal b/d	124	Irrecoverable	124

Task 8.2

A business which is registered for VAT has receivables of £16,475 at its year end of 30 September 20X8. The business's normal terms of trade are that payment from receivables is due within 30 days. On the basis of this it has been decided that two debts are to be written off as irrecoverable at the year end:

- £1,200 due from H Maguire
- £470 due from J Palmer

You are required to write off these irrecoverable debts in the general and sales ledger accounts given below showing any amounts to be charged to the statement of profit or loss for the year and the amended year end balances.

General ledger

Sales ledger control account

	£		£
Bal b/d	16475	Irrecoverable	1670
		Bal c/d	14805

Irrecoverable debts expense account

	£		£
SLCA	1670	SPL	1670

Sales ledger

H Maguire

	£		£
Bal b/d	1200	Irreco	1200

J Palmer

	£		£
Bal b/d	470	Irrecoverable	470

Task 8.3

In the year ended 31 December 20X7 a business wrote off a debt for £488 owed by one of its customers, R Trevor, as irrecoverable. At 31 December 20X8 the balance on its sales ledger control account was £7,264. Of this it was decided that a debt from E Ingham for £669 would be written off as irrecoverable. In the year to 31 December 20X8 the £488 from R Trevor was unexpectedly received.

You are required to write up the general and sales ledger accounts given below for the year ended 31 December 20X8 to reflect these facts.

General ledger

Sales ledger control account

	£		£
Bal b/d	7264	Irrecoverable	669
		Bal c/d	6595
	7264		7264

Irrecoverable debts expense account

	£		£
SLCA	669	Bank	488
		SPL	181

Sales ledger

R Trevor

	£		£

E Ingham

	£		£
Bal b/d	669	Irrecoverable	669

BPP
LEARNING MEDIA

Task 8.4

Marcham has a balance on the sales ledger control account as at 30 September 20X8 of £218,940. Marcham has identified that Hendrick will not be able to pay his balance of £2,440, and wishes to write this amount off. For the remaining receivables as at 30 September 20X8, Marcham wants to have an allowance for doubtful debts of 3% of the balance. At 1 October 20X7 Marcham's allowance for doubtful debts was £5,215.

Complete the sales ledger control account, the allowance for doubtful debts account, the irrecoverable debts expense account and the allowance for doubtful debts adjustment account, closing off the expense accounts to the statement of profit or loss and carrying down the balances on the statement of financial position accounts.

1280 +

Sales ledger control account

	£		£
Bal b/d	218,940	Irrecoverable	2440

Allowance for doubtful debts account

	£		£
		Bal b/d	5215
Bal c/d	6495	OD adj	1280

Irrecoverable debts expense account

	£		£
SLCA	2440	SPL	2440

Allowance for doubtful debts adjustment account

	£		£
OD	1280	SPL	1280

Task 8.5

An allowance for doubtful debts is an example of which accounting concept?

✓	
	Accruals
	Consistency
	Materiality
✓	Prudence

Chapter 9 – Bank reconciliations

Task 9.1

Albert has compared his cash book to the business bank statement for the month of May. He has identified a number of differences.

Prepare journal entries for the general ledger accounts or a note stating how it will be treated in the bank reconciliation statement, which ever is appropriate, for each of these items.

(a) Cheque number 10752, payable to a credit supplier, for £360 has been incorrectly entered in the cash book as £340.

Account name	Amount £	Debit (✓)	Credit (✓)

or

Note for bank reconciliation:

(b) Bank interest received on the bank statement of £45.

Account name	Amount £	Debit (✓)	Credit (✓)

or

Note for bank reconciliation:

(c) A BACs receipt from a customer for £5,400 has not been entered in the cash book,

Account name	Amount £	Debit (✓)	Credit (✓)

or

Note for bank reconciliation:

BPP LEARNING MEDIA

(d) Cheque number 10810 for £2,356 issued on 29 May, in respect of payment of an invoice for accountancy services, is not showing on the bank statement.

Account name	Amount £	Debit (✓)	Credit (✓)

or

Note for bank reconciliation:

Task 9.2

The following differences have been identified when reconciling the cash book to the bank statement for the month of June:

1. Bank charges of £25 were not entered in the cash book.

2. The bank made an error and processed a standing order for £500 which does not relate to the business.

3. A cheque received from a credit customer for £895 has been incorrectly entered in the cash book as £859.

4. A cheque received from a customer for £650, which was recorded in the cash book and paid into the bank on 30 June, is not showing on the bank statement.

Use the following table to show the adjustments, if any, you need to make to the general ledger to deal with the above differences.

Adjustment	Amount £	Debit ✓	Credit ✓

Task 9.3

Murrays Office Supplies' cash receipts and payments books for the week ending 7 July, the bank statement for that week and the bank reconciliation statement that was prepared for the week ended 30 June are set out below.

You are required to prepare the bank reconciliation statement for the week ending 7 July.

Bank reconciliation as at 7 July

	£
Balance per bank statement	
Add:	
Total to add:	
Less:	
Total to subtract:	
Balance as per cash book	

Cash Receipts Book

Date	Details	£
3 July	F Hald & Co	8,590.61
5 July	S Rose	485.21
5 July	W Field Suppliers	720.15
5 July	T Woods Manufacturing Ltd	6,351.25
6 July	R Forge	225.63
		16,372.85

BPP LEARNING MEDIA

Cash Payments Book

Date	Details	Cheque number	£
3 July	F W Stationers	003125	7,565.56
	A Ross & Co	003126	126.89
4 July	S Accountancy services	003127	500.00
	Grange Ltd	003128	896.78
	Wombat Supplies	003129	663.14
	Gas Suppliers	DD	1,100.00
5 July	Manor Garage	003130	105.45
7 July	Oberon Marketing	003131	4,325.00
			15,282.82

MAPLES BANK

19 Maple Square, Wallage, WA9 9PO

STATEMENT

Account Name:

Murrays Office Supplies

Account No: 71-20-21 85963245

Date	Details	DEBITS (Payments)	CREDITS (Receipts)	Balance
		£	£	£
1/7	Balance b/d			8,751.23 CR
3/7	Credit		2,875.45	11,626.68 CR
4/7	DD - Gas	1,100.00		10,526.68 CR
5/7	Cheque 3122	4,895.36		5,631.32 CR
6/7	BGC		6,351.25	
6/7	Cheque 3123	158.96		
6/7	Cheque 3125	7,565.56		4,258.05 CR
7/7	Credit		8,590.61	12,848.66 CR

Bank reconciliation statement at 30 June

	£	£
Balance per bank statement at 30 June		8,751.23
Less unpresented cheques		
003122	4,895.36	
003123	158.96	
003124	589.45	
		(5,643.77)
		3,107.46
Add outstanding lodgement		2,875.45
Balance as per cash book at 30 June		5,982.91

Task 9.4

Which of the following is not a valid reason for the cash book balance and the bank statement balance failing to agree?

✓	
	Timing difference
	Bank charges
	Error
	Cash receipts total posted to purchases ledger control account

BPP LEARNING MEDIA

Chapter 10 – Control account reconciliations

Task 10.1

Given below are summaries of transactions with receivables for the month of February for a business. The balance on the sales ledger control account at 1 February was £4,268.

	£
Credit sales	15,487
Sales returns	995
Irrecoverable debt written off	210
Cheques from receivables	13,486
Discounts allowed	408
Contra entry	150
Cheque returned 'refer to drawer'	645

You are required to write up the sales ledger control account showing the balance on 28 February.

Sales ledger control account

	£		£
Bal b/d	4268	Irreco	~~222~~ 210
Sales	15487	sales return	995
dishounred chqque	645	Bank	13486
		dis	408
		Contra	150

....

Task 10.2

The balance on the purchases ledger control account for a business at 1 February was £3,299. The transactions with payables for the month of February are summarised below:

	£
Credit purchases	12,376
Cheques to payables	10,379
Returns to suppliers	1,074
Discounts received	302
Contra entry	230

You are required to write up the purchases ledger control account for the month and to show the closing balance on 28 February.

Purchases ledger control account

	£		£

Task 10.3

Given below is a summary of a business's transactions with its receivables and payables during the month of May. The balances on the sales ledger and purchases ledger control accounts on 1 May were £12,634 and £10,553 respectively.

	£
Credit purchases	40,375
Credit sales	51,376
Cheques from customers	50,375
Discounts received	1,245
Sales returns	3,173
Cheques to suppliers	35,795
Purchases returns	2,003
Contra entry	630
Discounts allowed	1,569

You are required to write up the sales ledger and purchases ledger control accounts for the month of May showing the balances at the end of the month.

Sales ledger control account

	£		£

BPP
LEARNING MEDIA

Purchases ledger control account

	£		£

Task 10.4

At 31 March the balance on a business's sales ledger control account was £6,237 but the total of the list of balances from the sales ledger was £8,210. The following errors were discovered:

(a) The sales day book had been undercast by £1,000.

(b) The discounts allowed of £340 had been entered into the general ledger as £430. 90

(c) A contra entry of £123 had been made in the general ledger but not in the sales ledger.

(d) A credit note to a customer for £320 had been entered on the wrong side of the customer's account in the sales ledger.

(e) A credit balance of £60 had been included in the list of balances as a debit.

Use the following table to show the adjustments you need to make to the sales ledger control account.

Adjustment	Amount £	Debit ✓	Credit ✓
b	90	✓	
d	1000	✓	

Task 10.5

The balance on a business's purchases ledger control account at 31 January was £3,105 but the total of the list of balances from the purchases ledger was £1,850 at the same date. The following errors were discovered:

(a) The total from the purchases returns day book of £288 was entered on the wrong side of the control account.

(b) A contra entry for £169 was entered in the individual supplier's account but not in the general ledger.

(c) A purchase invoice for £350 was entered on the wrong side of the supplier's account in the purchases ledger.

(d) The total of the cash payments book was overcast by £100.

(e) A credit note to F Miller for £97 was entered into the account for A Miller.

(f) A balance of £780 was incorrectly listed as £870 when the purchases ledger balances were being totalled.

Use the following table to show the adjustments you need to make to the purchases ledger control account.

Adjustment	Amount £	Debit ✓	Credit ✓
a	576	✓	
b	169	✓	
d	100		✓

Task 10.6

An investigation reveals the following errors in a business's ledgers and day books.

(a) The invoice totals for the sales day book for January was overcast by £900.00.

(b) One invoice for £1,440.00 including VAT was duplicated in the sales day book for January.

(c) Cash received of £120.00 from Nelson Ltd was posted to the wrong side of its sales ledger account.

(d) The purchases column of the purchase day book for January was undercast by £270.00. Ignore VAT.

(e) One marketing invoice total for £872.00 including VAT was omitted from the purchase day book in January.

(f) An invoice totalling £1,092.35 was posted twice to the purchases ledger account of Harrier Ltd.

(g) A contra of £582.45 was made in the sales and purchases ledger accounts of Tremayne Holdings plc.

You are required to prepare journals to correct the general ledger accounts fully.

Account name	Debit £	Credit £
Being correction of errors in sales ledger control account		
Being correction of errors in purchases ledger control account		

Task 10.7

The total of the balances in a business's sales ledger is £1,000 more than the debit balance on its sales ledger control account.

Which one of the following errors could by itself account for the discrepancy?

✓	
✓	The sales day book has been undercast by £1,000
	Settlement discounts totalling £1,000 have been omitted from the general ledger
	One sales ledger account with a credit balance of £1,000 has been treated as a debit balance
	The cash receipts book has been undercast by £1,000

Task 10.8

When reconciling the purchases ledger control account to the list of balances on the purchases ledger, it was discovered that an invoice received from a supplier for £72 had been recorded in the purchases day book as £27.

What adjustment is necessary to the control account and the list of balances?

✓	Control account	List of balances
	Debit £45	Add £45
✓	Credit £45	Add £45
	Debit £45	Subtract £45
	Credit £45	Subtract £45

Task 10.9

What is the correct treatment of discounts allowed and discounts received?

✓	Discounts allowed	Discounts received
	Debit purchases ledger control	Credit sales ledger control
	Credit purchases ledger control	Credit sales ledger control
	Debit sales ledger control	Credit purchases ledger control
✓	Credit sales ledger control	Debit purchases ledger control

BPP
LEARNING MEDIA

Chapter 11 – The trial balance, errors and the suspense account

Task 11.1

For each of the following errors indicate whether there is an imbalance in the trial balance or not.

Error	Imbalance ✓	No imbalance ✓
The payment of the telephone bill was posted to the cash payments book and then credited to the telephone account	✓	
The depreciation expense was debited to the accumulated depreciation account and credited to the depreciation expense account		✓
The electricity account balance of £750 was taken to the trial balance as £570	✓	
The motor expenses were debited to the motor vehicles at cost account		✓
The discounts received in the cash payments book were not posted to the general ledger		✓

Task 11.2

A trial balance has been prepared for a business and the total of the debit balances is £228,678 and the total of the credits is £220,374.

What is the balance on the suspense account?

	Debit balance ✓	Credit balance ✓
£ 8304		✓

Task 11.3

Draft a journal entry to correct each of the following errors – narratives should be included.

(a) The telephone expense of £236 was debited to the electricity account.

Account name	Debit £	Credit £
Electricity		236
Telephone exp	236	

(b) A sales invoice for £645 was entered into the sales day book as £465.

Account name	Debit £	Credit £
Sales		✓180
SLCA	180	

(c) A credit note received from a supplier for £38 was omitted from the purchases returns day book.

Account name	Debit £	Credit £
PR		38
PLCA	38	

(d) The increase in allowance for doubtful debts of £127 was debited to the allowance for doubtful debts account and credited to the allowance for doubtful debts adjustment account.

Account name	Debit £	Credit £
DD		254
DD adj	254	

(e) A contra entry of £200 was debited to the sales ledger control account and credited to the purchases ledger control account.

Account name	Debit £	Credit £
PLCA	400	
SLCA		400

Task 11.4

A business has just drafted its trial balance and the debit balances exceed the credit balances by £1,370. A suspense account has been set up to record the difference and the following errors have been noted:

(a) The discounts allowed from the cash receipts book of £240 have not been posted to the general ledger.

(b) The sales ledger column in the cash receipts book totalling £2,700 were not posted to the sales ledger control account.

(c) The wages account balance of £74,275 was included in the trial balance as £72,475.

(d) An irrecoverable debt written off for £235 was debited to the sales ledger control account and debited to the irrecoverable debts expense account.

(e) A purchase invoice for £480 was entered into the purchases day book as £580.

You are required to set up the suspense account balance and then to clear it.

Suspense account

	£		£
SLCA	2700	Bal b/d	1370
SLCA	470	wages	1800

Task 11.5

When drawing up the trial balance at the end of the accounting year a suspense account debit balance of £3,100 was set up to account for the difference in the trial balance. The following errors were discovered:

(a) The payment of insurance premiums of £1,585 was correctly entered into the cash payments book and then credited to the insurance account.

(b) A payment for postage costs of £26 was posted from the petty cash book to the postage account as £62.

X (c) The total of the discounts allowed column in the cash receipts book was undercast by £100.

(d) The balance of £34 on the bank interest received account was omitted from the trial balance.

X (e) One page of the purchases returns day book totalling £130 was not posted to the general ledger.

You are required to set up the suspense account and then show how it is cleared.

Suspense account

	£		£
Bal b/d	3100	Insurance	3170
Postage	36		
Bank interest	34		
	3170		3170

Task 11.6

Shortly before the year end a business sold a non-current asset for £4,000. The bookkeeper entered the receipt in the cash receipts book but did not know what else to do and therefore credited a suspense account with the amount. The non-current asset sold had originally cost £15,000 and had accumulated depreciation charged to it at the date of sale of £10,500.

You are to draft a journal entry to correctly account for this disposal and to show how the suspense account is cleared.

Account name	Debit £	Credit £

Task 11.7

Refer to the information provided below, and prepare a journal to clear the Green Bottles Ltd's suspense account on which there is a credit balance of £1,641.38. ?

(i)   The balance of £43,529.18 brought down on the wages ledger account was miscast. The correct balance is £43,259.18.

(ii)   The balance of £25,131.14 brought down on the purchases ledger control account was miscast. The correct balance is £25,311.14.

(iii) Cash received of £891.20 from Lewis & Co was posted to the wrong side of its sales ledger account.

(iv)   One receipt for £1,191.38 was included in the cash book in March but was omitted from the total posted to the sales ledger control account.

Account name	Debit £	Credit £
	1641.38	

....

Task 11.8

List five different types of error in accounting transactions.

....

Task 11.9

When a trial balance was prepared, two ledger accounts were omitted.

Discounts received   £1,500

Discounts allowed   £1,000

The total of debit balances in the TB therefore | exceeds/falls below | **the total of credit balances by:**

£ 500

Task 11.10

When a trial balance was prepared, a suspense account was opened. It was discovered that the only error that had been made was to record £350 of discounts received on the wrong side of the trial balance.

What is the journal to correct this error?

✓			
	Debit	Discounts received	£350
	Credit	Suspense	£350
	Debit	Suspense	£350
	Credit	Discounts received	£350
	Debit	Discounts received	£700
	Credit	Suspense	£700
	Debit	Suspense	£700
	Credit	Discounts received	£700

Task 11.11

A sole trader has drafted his initial trial balance and found that the balance on the rent account is a debit of £3,600 and the balance on the insurance account is a debit of £4,250. Rent of £1,200 is due to be paid for the final quarter of the year and the insurance payments include £850 which relate to the following accounting period.

BPP LEARNING MEDIA

Write in the statement of profit or loss charges for:

	£
Rent	
Insurance	

. . . .

Task 11.12

Given below is the initial trial balance of a sole trader for his year ended 30 June 20X8.

	Debit £	Credit £
Administration expenses	7,250	
Cash at bank	3,280	
Capital		60,000
Distribution expenses	1,210	
Purchases ledger control		1,530
Sales ledger control	20,200	
Discounts allowed	16,840	
Discounts received		
Drawings	14,600	
Machinery at cost	58,400	
Motor vehicles at cost	22,100	
Purchases	105,040	
Allowance for doubtful debts		300
Accumulated depreciation – machinery		23,360
– motor vehicles		9,680
Sales		186,070
Inventory at 1 July 20X7	15,400	
Selling expenses	5,800	
VAT owed to HMRC		3,690
Wages	16,700	
Suspense		330
	286,820	286,820

Since drawing up the initial trial balance a number of errors have been discovered:

(i) Selling expenses of £340 paid by cheque have been omitted from the accounts completely.

(ii) Purchases of £180 were entered on the wrong side of the account although the entry to the bank account was correctly made.

(iii) Discounts allowed of £690 were credited to receivables and debited to both the discounts allowed account and the discounts received account.

There are also a number of year end adjustments which have yet to be accounted for:

(iv) The closing inventory at 30 June 20X8 has been valued at £18,200.

(v) An irrecoverable debt of £2,800 is to be written off and an allowance of 2% is to be maintained of the remaining receivables.

(vi) Invoices for administration expenses for June 20X8 totalling £680 were not received until after the trial balance had been drawn up.

(vii) Included in administration expenses are payments of £440 which relate to the period after 30 June 20X8.

(viii) Depreciation has not yet been charged for the year. The machinery is depreciated at 20% per annum straight line and the motor vehicles are depreciated on the diminishing balance basis at a rate of 25%.

You are required to draft journal entries to correct the errors found and put through the year end adjustments.

Account name	Debit £	Credit £
Selling EXP	340	
Bank		340
Purchase	360	
Suspense		360
Dis received		690
Suspense	690	
Inventory SPL		18200
intory SoFP	18200	
DD Adj	48	
OD		48
Irre	2800	
SLCA		2800
Admin exp a/c	680	
accrued exp		680
Prepayment	440	
admin exp		440

Task 11.13

When a trial balance was prepared, two ledger accounts were omitted:

Discounts received   £6,150

Discounts allowed   £7,500

To make the trial balance balance, a suspense account was opened.

What was the balance on the suspense account?

✓	
	Debit £1,350
	Credit £1,350
	Debit £13,650
	Credit £13,650

Task 11.14

The suspense account shows a debit balance of £100. This could be due to:

✓	
	Entering £50 received from A Turner on the debit side of A Turner's account
	Entering £50 received from A Turner on the credit side of A Turner's account
	Undercasting the sales day book by £100
	Undercasting the sales ledger account by £100

BPP LEARNING MEDIA

Chapter 12 – The extended trial balance

Task 12.1

A sole trader has balanced off his ledger accounts as at 31 May 20X8 and has now asked for your help in producing his financial statements.

(a) **Draw up and total the initial trial balance, inserting a balance for the suspense account as required.**

		Initial trial balance		Adjustments	
	£	Debit £	Credit £	Debit £	Credit £
Accumulated depreciation					
– furniture and fittings	6,100		6100		
– motor vehicles	22,000		22000		
Accrued expenses					
Allowance for doubtful debts	1,000		1000		
Allowance for doubtful debts adjustment					
Bank overdraft	1,650		1650		
Capital	74,000		74000		
Depreciation expense – furniture & fittings					
Depreciation expense – motor vehicles					
Discounts allowed	2,100	2100			
Discounts received	1,800		1800		
Drawings	30,000	30000			
Electricity	2,300	2300			
Furniture and fittings at cost	24,500	24500			
Insurance	3,000	3000			

	£	Initial trial balance Debit £	Initial trial balance Credit £	Adjustments Debit £	Adjustments Credit £
Irrecoverable debts expense					
Miscellaneous expenses	1,200	1200			
Motor expenses	3,400	3400			
Motor vehicles at cost	48,000	48000			
Prepayments					
Purchases	245,000	245000			
Purchases ledger control	40,800		40800		
Rent paid	4,200	4200			
Sales	369,000		369000		
Sales ledger control	61,500	61500			
Inventory	41,000	41000			
Suspense					
Telephone	1,600	1600			
VAT due to HMRC	4,100		4100		
Wages	52,000	52000			

(b) A number of year end adjustments have yet to be made to the trial balance figures:

(i) Inventory at 31 May 20X8 has been valued at £43,500.

(ii) The balances for accumulated depreciation are as at 1 June 20X7. Depreciation is to be provided at 30% on the diminishing balance method on motor vehicles and at 10% straight line on the furniture and fittings.

(iii) It has been decided that an irrecoverable debt of £1,500 should be written off and that the allowance for doubtful debts is to remain at 2% of remaining receivables.

(iv) There are accruals of £650 of electricity and £350 of telephone.

(v) Rent of £800 has already been paid for the quarter ended 31 August 20X8 and insurance includes £1,200 for the year ended 31 December 20X8.

BPP LEARNING MEDIA

You are required to draft the journal entries required for these year end adjustments.

Account name	Debit £	Credit £
Inventory SPL		43500
~ ~ SoFP	43500	

(c) Since the drafting of the initial trial balance a number of errors have come to light:

    (i)   Motor expenses have been charged with £300 of miscellaneous expenses.

    (ii)   Discounts allowed of £425 and discounts received of £100 had been entered on the wrong side of the respective discounts accounts.

You are required to draft the journal entries needed to correct these errors.

Account name	Debit £	Credit £

(d) Put through the year end adjustments and the corrections of the errors in the adjustments column in (a) above and check that the two columns cast.

Task 12.2

Given below is the list of balances for a business at its year end of 31 May 20X8.

	£
Inventory at 1 June 20X7	1,600
Motor vehicles at cost	23,800
Computer at cost	2,400
Furniture and fittings at cost	12,800
Accumulated depreciation at 1 June 20X7:	
Motor vehicles	12,140
Computer	600
Furniture and fittings	2,560
Wages	16,400
Telephone	900
Electricity	1,200
Advertising	400
Stationery	600
Motor expenses	1,700
Miscellaneous expenses	300
Insurance	1,000
Sales	86,400
Purchases	38,200
Sales ledger control account	7,200
Allowance for doubtful debts at 1 June 20X7	200
Bank (debit balance)	1,300
Petty cash	100
Purchases ledger control account	3,180
VAT (credit balance)	960
Capital	25,000
Drawings	21,140

BPP LEARNING MEDIA

You are also provided with the following information:

(i) The depreciation charge for the year has not yet been accounted for:

- Motor vehicles are to be depreciated at 30% on the diminishing balance basis

- The computer is being depreciated at 25% on the straight-line basis

- The furniture and fittings are being depreciated at 20% on the straight-line basis

(ii) There is an accrual for electricity expenses of £400.

(iii) There is £300 of prepaid insurance.

(iv) The allowance for doubtful debts is to be 4% of the year end receivables.

(v) £100 of advertising costs have been included in the stationery account.

(vi) The closing inventory has been valued at £2,100.

You are required to:

(a) **Enter the initial balances onto the extended trial balance given and check that the trial balance does balance.**

(b) **Enter each of the adjustments into the adjustments columns on the extended trial balance and total the adjustments columns.**

(c) **Extend the figures into the statement of profit or loss and statement of financial position columns, and total the columns including calculating the profit and entering it into the statement of financial position columns.**

Account name	Ledger balance		Adjustments		SPL		SFP	
	Debit £	Credit £	Debit £	Credit £	Debit £	Credit £	Debit £	Credit £
Inventory at 1 June 20X7								
Motor vehicles at cost								
Computer at cost								
Furniture and fittings at cost								
Accumulated depreciation at 1 June 20X7:								
Motor vehicles								
Computer								
Furniture and fittings								
Wages								
Telephone								
Electricity								
Advertising								
Stationery								
Motor expenses								
Miscellaneous expenses								
Insurance								
Sales								
Purchases								
Sales ledger control								
Allowance for doubtful debts at 1 June 20X7								
Bank (debit balance)								
Petty cash								
Purchases ledger control								

Account name	Ledger balance		Adjustments		SPL		SFP	
	Debit £	Credit £	Debit £	Credit £	Debit £	Credit £	Debit £	Credit £
VAT (credit balance)								
Capital								
Drawings								
Depreciation expense:								
Motor vehicles								
Computer								
Furniture and fittings								
Accruals								
Prepayments								
Allowance for doubtful debts adjustment								
Profit / loss								

Task 12.3

Given below is the list of balances for a business at the end of June 20X8.

	£
Capital	150,000
Purchases ledger control	40,400
Sales ledger control	114,500
Sales	687,000
Inventory at 1 July 20X7	40,400
Machinery at cost	68,000
Furniture and fittings at cost	32,400
Wages	98,700
Sales returns	4,800
Telephone	4,100
Purchases	485,000
Heat and light	3,400
Advertising	8,200
Purchases returns	3,000
Selling costs	9,400
Discounts received	4,700
Discounts allowed	3,900
Administrative expenses	14,800
Miscellaneous expense	400
Accumulated depreciation at 1 July 20X7:	
Plant and machinery	34,680
Furniture and fittings	6,480
Allowance for doubtful debts at 1 July 20X7	2,000
Drawings	36,860
Bank (debit balance)	6,400
VAT (credit balance)	3,200
Suspense account (debit balance)	200

BPP
LEARNING MEDIA

You are also given the following information:

(a) The depreciation charges for the year are to be accounted for:

    (i) Depreciation on machinery is at the rate of 30% diminishing balance.

    (ii) Depreciation on furniture and fittings is at the rate of 20% straight line.

(b) The suspense account balance has been investigated and the following errors have been discovered:

    (i) Discounts received of £450 had been posted to the purchases ledger control account but not to the discount account.

    (ii) Sales returns of £480 were correctly posted to the sales ledger control account but were posted as £840 in the sales returns account.

    (iii) A subtotal in the cash payments book of £1,010 for heat and light was not posted to the heat and light account.

(c) An irrecoverable debt of £1,500 is to be written off and an allowance of 2% of receivables is required.

(d) There is an accrual for telephone expenses of £400 and the administrative expenses include prepaid amounts of £700.

(e) Closing inventory has been valued at £42,800.

You are required to:

(a) **Enter the ledger balances (including the suspense account) onto the extended trial balance given and total the trial balance to ensure that it agrees.**

(b) **Enter the adjustments in the adjustments columns and total them.**

(c) **Extend the extended trial balance into the statement of profit or loss and statement of financial position columns, total the columns to find the profit or loss and extend this into the statement of financial position columns.**

Account name	Ledger balance		Adjustments		SPL		SFP	
	Debit £	Credit £	Debit £	Credit £	Debit £	Credit £	Debit £	Credit £
Capital								
Purchases ledger control								
Sales ledger control								
Sales								
Inventory at 1 June 20X7:								
Machinery at cost								
Furniture and fittings at cost								
Wages								
Sales returns								
Telephone								
Purchases								
Heat and light								
Advertising								
Purchases returns								
Selling costs								
Discount received								
Discount allowed								
Administrative expenses								
Miscellaneous expense								
Accumulated depreciation at 1 July 20X7								
Machinery								
Furniture and fittings								

BPP LEARNING MEDIA

Account name	Ledger balance		Adjustments		SPL		SFP	
	Debit £	Credit £	Debit £	Credit £	Debit £	Credit £	Debit £	Credit £
Allowance for doubtful debts at 1 July 20X7								
Drawings								
Bank (debit balance)								
VAT (credit balance)								
Suspense account								
Depreciation expense:								
Machinery								
Furniture and fittings								
Allowance for doubtful debts adjustment								
Accruals								
Prepayments								
Profit / loss								

Task 12.4

Below is an alphabetical list of balances taken from the ledger of Clegg and Co, a sole trader, as at 31 May 20X8. You are also provided with some additional information.

	£
Administration costs	72,019.27
Bank overdraft	8,290.12
Capital	50,000.00
Loan	100,000.00
Depreciation charge	12,000.00
Drawings	36,000.00
Motor vehicles: cost	120,287.00
Motor vehicles: accumulated depreciation	36,209.28
Interest charges	12,182.26
Interest income	21.00
Wages	167,302.39
Purchases	104,293.38
Inventory as at 1 June 20X7	25,298.30
Purchases ledger control	42,190.85
Sales	481,182.20
Sales ledger control	156,293.00
VAT payable	4,938.20

(a) **Enter the balances in the format trial balance provided below. Set up a suspense account if necessary.**

(b) **With reference to the additional information below, clear the suspense account.**

(i) The debit side of the journal to record depreciation expense of £15,000.00 for the second six months of the period has been omitted.

(ii) An examination of administration costs shows that there is a prepayment for insurance of £320.00 and an accrual for electricity of £480.00.

(iii) One page of the sales returns day book was left out of the total posted to the sales ledger control account, although it was included in the other totals posted. The total value of credit notes on this page was £6,092.35.

(iv) Invoices totalling £6,283.38 have not been recorded in the purchases ledger accounts.

(v) The payment by BACS of wages in May of £14,248.40 has not been posted to the wages account, and nor has the purchase in May of a non-current asset for £4,000.00 been posted. This asset should be depreciated at a rate of 25% straight line, with a full year's depreciation being charged in the year of purchase.

(vi) A cash receipt of £10,000.00 was recorded in the cash book but, as it was not identified, it has not yet been posted. It has now been clarified that this represents additional capital from the owner.

(vii) Interest due of £650.00 on the loan needs to be accrued.

(viii) At 31 May 20X8 inventory on hand was valued at £32,125.28.

(c) **With reference to the additional information above, make whatever other adjustments to the trial balance are necessary.**

(d) (i) **Extend the trial balance**

    (ii) **Total all columns of the extended trial balance.**

    (iii) **Make entries to record the profit or loss for the year ended 31 May 20X8.**

Account name	Trial balance		Adjustments		SPL		SFP	
	Debit £	Credit £	Debit £	Credit £	Debit £	Credit £	Debit £	Credit £
Administration costs								
Bank overdraft								
Capital								
Loan								
Depreciation charge								
Drawings								
Motor vehicles: Cost								
Motor vehicles: Depreciation								
Interest: paid								
Interest: received								
Wages								
Raw materials								
Inventory as at 1/6/X7								
Purchases ledger control								
Sales								
Sales ledger control								
Suspense								
VAT payable								
Accruals								
Prepayments								
Closing inventory								
Profit / loss								

Task 12.5

When an extended trial balance is extended and a business has made a profit, this figure for profit will be in the | debit/credit | column of the statement of profit or loss.

Task 12.6

What is the double entry to record closing inventory on the ETB?

	Account name
Debit	
Credit	

Task 12.7

Which of these statements is/are correct?

(i)   A casting error in a day book will stop the trial balance balancing.

(ii) A transposition error in a daybook will stop the trial balance balancing.

✔	
	(i) only
	(i) and (ii)
	(ii) only
	Neither (i) or (ii)

Task 12.8

When a trial balance was prepared, two ledger accounts were omitted:

    Discounts received   £2,050

    Discounts allowed   £2,500

To make the trial balance balance a suspense account was opened.

What was the balance on the suspense account?

✓	
	Debit £450
	Credit £450
	Debit £4,550
	Credit £4,550

Answer bank

Chapter 1

Task 1.1

The sales returns day book lists	credit notes sent to customers
The purchases day book lists	invoices received from suppliers
The purchases returns day book lists	credit notes received from suppliers
The sales day book lists	invoices sent to customers

Task 1.2

What are the two effects of each of these transactions for accounting purposes?

Transaction	Account 1			Account 2		
	Name	Increase ✓	Decrease ✓	Name	Increase ✓	Decrease ✓
Payment of £15,000 into a business bank account by an individual in order to start up a business	bank	✓		capital	✓	
Payment by cheque of £2,000 for rent of a business property	bank		✓	rent expense	✓	
Payment by cheque of £6,200 for purchase of a delivery van	bank		✓	non-current asset	✓	
Payment by cheque of £150 for vehicle licence for the van	bank		✓	van expenses	✓	
Payment by cheque of £2,100 for goods for resale	bank		✓	purchases	✓	
Sale of goods for cash and cheques of £870	bank	✓		sales	✓	
Purchase of goods for resale on credit for £2,800	purchases	✓		purchases ledger control	✓	

Transaction	Account 1			Account 2		
	Name	Increase ✓	Decrease ✓	Name	Increase ✓	Decrease ✓
Payment by cheque for petrol of £80	bank		✓	van expenses	✓	
Sale of goods on credit for £3,400	sales	✓		sales ledger control	✓	
Payment by cheque of £1,500 to credit suppliers	bank		✓	purchases ledger control		✓
Payment by cheque of electricity bill of £140	bank		✓	electricity expense	✓	
Receipt of cheque from credit customer of £1,600	bank	✓		sales ledger control		✓
Withdrawal of £500 of cash for the owner's personal living costs	bank		✓	drawings	✓	
Payment by cheque for petrol of £70	bank		✓	van expenses	✓	

Task 1.3

Capital account

	£		£
		Bank	15,000

BPP LEARNING MEDIA

Bank account

	£		£
Capital	15,000	Rent	2,000
Sales	870	Van	6,200
Sales ledger control	1,600	Van expenses	150
		Purchases	2,100
		Van expenses	80
		Purchases ledger control	1,500
		Electricity	140
		Drawings	500
		Van expenses	70
		Balance c/d	4,730
			17,470
	17,470		
Balance b/d	4,730		

Rent account

	£		£
Bank	2,000		

Van account

	£		£
Bank	6,200		

Van expenses account

	£		£
Bank	150		
Bank	80		
Bank	70	Balance c/d	300
	300		300
Balance b/d	300		

Purchases account

	£		£
Bank	2,100		
Purchases ledger control	2,800	Balance c/d	4,900
	4,900		4,900
Balance b/d	4,900		

Sales account

	£		£
		Bank	870
Balance c/d	4,270	Sales ledger control	3,400
	4,270		4,270
		Balance b/d	4,270

Purchases ledger control account

	£		£
Bank	1,500	Purchases	2,800
Balance c/d	1,300		
	2,800		2,800
		Balance b/d	1,300

Sales ledger control account

	£		£
Sales	3,400	Bank	1,600
		Balance c/d	1,800
	3,400		3,400
Balance b/d	1,800		

BPP
LEARNING MEDIA

Electricity account

	£		£
Bank	140		

Drawings account

	£		£
Bank	500		

Trial balance	Debit £	Credit £
Capital		15,000
Bank	4,730	
Rent	2,000	
Van	6,200	
Van expenses	300	
Purchases	4,900	
Sales		4,270
Payables ie purchases ledger control account		1,300
Receivables ie sales ledger control account	1,800	
Electricity	140	
Drawings	500	
	20,570	20,570

Task 1.4

	An asset or an expense
	A liability or an expense
	An amount owing to the organisation
✓	A liability or a revenue item

Chapter 2

Task 2.1

(a)

Principle/concept	Materiality

(b)

Principle/concept	Going concern

(c)

Principle/concept	Accruals or matching

Task 2.2

Relevance	and	Faithful representation

Task 2.3

	Non-current assets ✓	Current assets ✓	Liabilities ✓
A PC used in the accounts department of a retail store	✓		
A PC on sale in an office equipment shop		✓	
Wages due to be paid to staff at the end of the week			✓
A van for sale in a motor dealer's showroom		✓	
A delivery van used in a grocer's business	✓		
An amount owing to a bank for a loan for the acquisition of a van, to be repaid over 9 months			✓

BPP LEARNING MEDIA

Chapter 3

Task 3.1

	Capital expenditure £	Revenue expenditure £
An SN63 sanding machine has been purchased at a cost of £12,000 plus VAT. The delivery charge was £400. After its initial run it was cleaned at a cost of £100.	12,400	100
A building has been purchased at a cost of £120,000. The surveyor's fees were an additional £400 and the legal fees £1,200. The building has been re-decorated at a total cost of £13,000. Ignore VAT.	121,600	13,000
A new main server has been purchased at a cost of £10,600. In order to house the server a room in the building has had to have a special air conditioning unit fitted at a cost of £2,450. The server's cost includes software worth £1,000 and CDs with a value of £100. Ignore VAT.	12,950	100
A salesperson's car has been purchased at a cost of £14,000 plus VAT. The invoice also shows delivery costs of £50 (plus VAT) and road fund licence of £160 (no VAT charged). The car is not available for private use by the salesperson.	14,050	160

Notes.

(1) The computer software could be treated as either capital or revenue expenditure. As the cost is quite large it would probably be treated as capital expenditure. The total capital expenditure is therefore £10,600 – 100 + 2,450 = £12,950.

(2) VAT is not included in the purchase price unless the car is available for private use. The amount of expenditure which is capitalised is therefore £14,000 plus the delivery costs of £50.

Task 3.2

The SPK100 repairs would be treated as:

✓	
	capital expenditure
✓	revenue expenditure

The FL11 repairs would be treated as:

	✓	
✓	capital expenditure	
	revenue expenditure	

Task 3.3

(a)

	Debit £	Credit £
Motor vehicles account	12,000	
VAT account (12,000 x 20%)	2,400	
Motor expenses account	150	
Bank account		14,550

(b)

	Debit £	Credit £
Machinery account (15,400 + 1,400)	16,800	
VAT account (15,400 × 0.20)	3,080	
Purchases ledger control account (15,400 + 3,080)		18,480
Wages account		1,400

(c)

	Debit £	Credit £
Computer account (3,800 – 150)	3,650	
Computer expenses account	150	
VAT account (3,800 × 20%)	760	
Bank account (3,800 + 760)		4,560

BPP LEARNING MEDIA

(d)

	Debit £	Credit £
Building maintenance account	800	
Bank account		800

(e)

	Debit £	Credit £
Computer expenses account	200	
Bank account		200

Task 3.4

Machinery account

	£		£
Balance b/d	103,400.00		
Bank	13,500.00		
Wages	400.00		
Purchases	850.00		

Buildings account

	£		£
Balance b/d	200,000.00		
Bank (150,000 + 20,000)	170,000.00		

VAT account

	£		£
Bank: VAT on machinery	2,700.00	Balance b/d	13,289.60
(13,500 × 20%)			

Purchases account

	£		£
Balance b/d	56,789.50	Machinery	850.00

Wages account

	£		£
Balance b/d	113,265.88	Machinery	400.00

Buildings maintenance account

	£		£
Balance b/d	10,357.00		
Bank	4,000.00		

Bank account

	£		£
Balance b/d	214,193.60	Machinery & VAT	
		(13,500 + 2,700)	16,200.00
		Buildings	170,000.00
		Buildings maintenance	4,000.00

Task 3.5

✓	True
	False

Task 3.6

Which of the following costs would be classified as capital expenditure for a restaurant business?

	A replacement for a broken window
	Repainting the restaurant
✓	An illuminated sign advertising the business name
	Knives and forks for the restaurant

Replacing a broken window is a repair, so it is revenue expenditure. Repainting the restaurant is a repair and renewal expense so this too is revenue. Knives and forks are not likely to be expensive enough to be treated as capital expenditure.

BPP
LEARNING MEDIA

Task 3.7

✓	
	On non-current assets, including repairs and maintenance
	On expensive assets
✓	Relating to the acquisition or improvement of non-current assets
	Incurred by the chief officer of the business

Improvements are capital expenditure, repairs and maintenance are not.

Chapter 4

Task 4.1

Accruals or matching

Task 4.2

	Workings	Depreciation charge £	Carrying amount £
Machine purchased for £17,400 on 1 January 20X6 with a useful life of 5 years and a zero residual value.	£17,400/5 years £17,400 – (3 × 3,480)	3,480	 6,960
Machine purchased for £12,800 on 1 January 20X7 with a useful life of 4 years and a residual value of £2,000.	$\dfrac{12,800 - 2,000}{4 \text{ years}}$ £12,800 – (2 × 2,700)	2,700	 7,400
Computer purchased for £4,600 on 1 January 20X8 with a useful life of 3 years and an estimated resale value of £700.	$\dfrac{4,600 - 700}{3 \text{ years}}$ £4,600 – 1,300	1,300	 3,300

Task 4.3

	Workings	Depreciation charge £	Carrying amount £
Machinery costing £24,600 purchased on 1 April 20X8 which is to be depreciated at 20% on the diminishing balance basis.	£24,600 × 20% £24,600 – £4,920	4,920	 19,680
Motor vehicle costing £18,700 purchased on 1 April 20X6 which is to be depreciated at 20% on the diminishing balance basis.	Y/e 31/3/X7: 18,700 × 20% = 3,740 18,700 – 3,740 = 14,960 Y/e 31/3/X8: 14,960 × 20% = 2,992 14,960 – 2,992 = 11,968 Y/e 31/3/X9: 11,968 × 20% = 2,394 11,968 – 2,394 = 9,574	 2,394	 9,574
Computer costing £3,800 purchased on 1 April 20X7 which is to be depreciated at 30% on the diminishing balance basis.	Y/e 31/3/X8: 3,800 × 30% = 1,140 3,800 – 1,140 = 2,660 Y/e 31/3/X9: 2,660 × 30% = 798 2,660 – 798 = 1,862	 798	 1,862

Task 4.4

	Workings	Depreciation charge £
Machine purchased on 1 May 20X8 for £14,000. This is to be depreciated at the rate of 20% per annum on the straight-line basis.	£14,000 × 20% × 8/12	1,866.67
Office furniture and fittings purchased on 1 June 20X8 for £3,200. These are to be depreciated on the diminishing balance basis at a rate of 25% with a full year's charge in the year of purchase and no charge in the year of disposal.	£3,200 × 25%	800.00
Computer purchased on 31 October 20X8 for £4,400. This is to be depreciated at the rate of 40% per annum on the straight-line basis.	£4,400 × 40% × 2/12	293.33

Task 4.5

	Workings	Depreciation charge £
20X0	1,800 × 60%	1,080
20X1	(1,800 – 1,080) × 60%	432
20X2	(1,800 – 1,080 – 432) × 60%	173
20X3	(1,800 – 1,080 – 432 – 173) × 60%	69

Task 4.6

Debit	Depreciation charge account
Credit	Accumulated depreciation account

BPP
LEARNING MEDIA

Task 4.7

	£605
✓	£363
	£179
	£72

Workings

	£
Cost	2,800
Depreciation to 31 Dec X4 (2,800 × 40%)	1,120
Carrying amount at 31 Dec X4	1,680
Depreciation to 31 Dec X5 (1,680 × 40%)	672
Carrying amount at 31 Dec X5	1,008
Depreciation to 31 Dec X6 (1,008 × 40%)	403
Carrying amount at 31 Dec X6	605
Depreciation to 31 Dec X7 (605 × 40%)	242
Carrying amount at 31 Dec X7	363

Task 4.8

✓	To allocate the cost less residual value of a non-current asset over the accounting periods expected to benefit from its use
	To ensure that funds are available for the eventual replacement of the asset
	To reduce the cost of the asset to its estimated market value
	To recognise the fact that assets lose their value over time

Chapter 5

Task 5.1

loss	of £	125

Workings

		£
1 Apr 20X7	Cost	12,500
31 Mar 20X8	Depreciation	(3,750)
Carrying amount		8,750
31 Mar 20X9	Depreciation	(2,625)
Carrying amount		6,125
Proceeds		(6,000)
Loss on disposal		125

Task 5.2

Workings

$$\text{Annual depreciation charge} = \frac{£25,000 - 3,000}{5}$$

$$= £4,400$$

Non-current asset at cost account

	£		£
1 Jan 20X6 Bank	25,000	31 Dec 20X8 Disposal	25,000

Depreciation account

	£		£
31 Dec 20X6 Accumulated depreciation	4,400	31 Dec 20X6 Statement of profit or loss	4,400
31 Dec 20X7 Accumulated depreciation	4,400	31 Dec 20X7 Statement of profit or loss	4,400
31 Dec 20X8 Accumulated depreciation	4,400	31 Dec 20X8 Statement of profit or loss	4,400

BPP LEARNING MEDIA

Accumulated depreciation account

	£		£
31 Dec 20X7 Balance c/d	8,800	31 Dec 20X6 Expense	4,400
		31 Dec 20X7 Expense	4,400
	8,800		8,800
31 Dec 20X8 Disposal	13,200	1 Jan 20X8 Balance b/d	8,800
		31 Dec 20X8 Expense	4,400
	13,200		13,200

Disposal account

	£		£
31 Dec 20X8 Cost	25,000	31 Dec 20X8 Accumulated depreciation	13,200
		31 Dec 20X8 Bank	11,000
		31 Dec 20X8 Statement of profit or loss	800
	25,000		25,000

Task 5.3

		£
1 Apr 20X7	Cost	13,800
31 Mar 20X8	Depreciation	(4,140)
Carrying amount		9,660
31 Mar 20X9	Depreciation	(2,898)
Carrying amount		6,762

Depreciation expense account

	£		£
31 Mar 20X9 Acc dep	2,898		

Accumulated depreciation account

	£		£
31 Mar 20X9 Disposal	7,038	1 Apr 20X8 Balance b/d	4,140
		31 Mar 20X9 Expense	2,898
	7,038		7,038

Motor vehicle at cost account

	£		£
1 Apr 20X8 Balance b/d	13,800	31 Mar 20X9 Disposal	13,800

Disposal account

	£		£
31 Mar 20X9 Cost	13,800	31 Mar 20X9 Acc dep	7,038
31 Mar 20X9 Profit	238	31 Mar 20X9 Bank	7,000
	14,038		14,038

Task 5.4

Disposal account

	£		£
30 Nov 20X8 Cost	15,600	30 Nov 20X8 Acc dep	9,425
		30 Nov 20X8 Bank	6,000
		30 Nov 20X8 Loss – SPL	175
	15,600		15,600

Workings

Depreciation at the date of disposal:

		£
31 December 20X6	$15,600 \times 25\% \times 6/12$	1,950
31 December 20X7	$15,600 \times 25\%$	3,900
31 December 20X8	$15,600 \times 25\% \times 11/12$	3,575
		9,425

Task 5.5

✓	
	Profit of £600
	Loss of £600
	Profit of £350
✓	Loss of £400

Workings

(£5,000 cost – £1,000 residual value) / 4 = £1,000 depreciation per annum. Carrying amount on disposal was therefore £2,000.

BPP
LEARNING MEDIA

Chapter 6

Task 6.1

Telephone account

	£		£
31 Mar Bank	845	31 Mar SPL	1,015
31 Mar Balance c/d	170		
	1,015		1,015

Task 6.2

Electricity account

	£		£
30 June Bank	2,300	30 June SPL	3,200
30 June Balance c/d	900		
	3,200		3,200

Task 6.3

Insurance account

	£		£
31 May Bank	2,300	31 May Balance c/d	250
		31 May SPL	2,050
	2,300		2,300

Task 6.4

Rent account

	£		£
30 June Bank	4,500	30 June Balance c/d	400
		30 June SPL	4,100
	4,500		4,500

BPP
LEARNING MEDIA

Task 6.5

Rental income account

	£		£
30 June Income in advance c/d	350	30 June Bank	5,600
30 June SPL	5,250		
	5,600		5,600

Task 6.6

✓	
	Overstated by £375
	Overstated by £750
	Understated by £375
✓	Understated by £750

An accrual of £375 should have been set up, which would have increased the electricity expense for the year by £375. Instead a prepayment was set up, decreasing the expense by £375. Setting up the prepayment instead of an accrual has therefore understated the expense for the year by £750 (2 × £375).

Task 6.7

£	18,388.23

	£
Paid in year	14,060.55
Accrual (2/3 × £6,491.52)	4,327.68
	18,388.23

BPP
LEARNING MEDIA

Task 6.8

£	900

Workings

Rent payable

20X1		£	20X1		£
31 Dec	Bank	1,275	1 Jan	Balance b/d	250
			31 Dec	Balance c/d (1/3 × £375)	125
				Statement of profit or loss	900
		1,275			1,275

Task 6.9

✓	
	£4,000
✓	£4,500
	£5,000
	£5,500

Working

Rental income account

	£		£
Balance b/d	1,000	Bank	5,000
Statement of profit or loss	4,500	Balance c/d	500
	5,500		5,500

Chapter 7

Task 7.1

£	25.10 (£24.60 + £0.5)

Net realisable value

£	24.80 (£25.80 – £1)

Value in the extended trial balance

£	3,100 (125 × £24.80)

Task 7.2

Inventory line	Quantity – units	Cost £	Selling price £	Selling costs £	Value per unit £	Total value £
A	180	12.50	20.40	0.50	12.50	2,250
B	240	10.90	12.60	1.80	10.80	2,592
C	300	15.40	22.70	1.20	15.40	4,620
D	80	16.50	17.80	1.50	16.30	1,304
E	130	10.60	18.00	1.00	10.60	1,378
						12,144

Task 7.3

		£
(a)	the FIFO method	435
(b)	the AVCO method	432

BPP
LEARNING MEDIA

Workings

(a) FIFO

Opening balance		80 units @ 8.20
Purchases		100 units @ 8.50
Sales	80 units @ 8.20	
	60 units @ 8.50	
	140 units	
	80 units @ 8.20	
Purchases		180 units @ 8.70
Sales	40 units @ 8.50	
	60 units @ 8.70	
	100 units	
Sales	70 units @ 8.70	
Closing inventory	50 units @ 8.70	£435.00

(b) AVCO

	Average cost	Quantity	Value £
Opening balance	8.20	80	656
Purchases	8.50	100	850
	8.37	180	1,506
Sales	8.37	(140)	(1,172)
		40	334
Sales	8.70	180	1,566
	8.64	220	1,900
Sales	8.64	(100)	(864)
Sales	8.64	(70)	(604)
	8.64	50	432

....

Task 7.4

> **The lower of cost and net realisable value**

....

Task 7.5

£	10,405

Workings

The settlement discount is irrelevant here.

	Cost less 2½% trade discount	NRV	Valuation
	£	£	£
Product A	3,510.00	5,100.00	3,510.00
Product B	2,827.50	2,800.00	2,800.00
Product C	4,095.00	4,100.00	4,095.00
			10,405.00

Task 7.6

	✓	
		The expected selling price of the inventory
	✓	The expected selling price less disposal costs
		The replacement cost of the inventory
		The market price

Net realisable value is the amount that can be obtained, less any further expenses incurred to bring the inventory to a condition in which it can be sold.

BPP
LEARNING MEDIA

Chapter 8

Task 8.1

General ledger

Sales ledger control account

	£		£
Balance b/d	5,479	Irrecoverable debts expense (321 + 124)	445
		Balance c/d	5,034
	5,479		5,479
Balance b/d	5,034		

Irrecoverable debts expense account

	£		£
Sales ledger control	445	Statement of profit or loss	445

Sales ledger

G Simms & Co

	£		£
Balance b/d	321	Irrecoverable debts	321

L Fitzgerald

	£		£
Balance b/d	124	Irrecoverable debts	124

Task 8.2

General ledger

Sales ledger control account

	£		£
30 Sep Balance b/d	16,475	30 Sep Irrecoverable debts expense (1,200 + 470)	1,670
		30 Sep Balance c/d	14,805
	16,475		16,475

Irrecoverable debts expense account

	£		£
30 Sep Sales ledger control	1,670	30 Sep SPL	1,670

Sales ledger

H Maguire

	£		£
30 Sep Balance b/d	1,200	30 Sep Irrecoverable debts	1,200

J Palmer

	£		£
30 Sep Balance b/d	470	30 Sep Irrecoverable debts	470

Task 8.3

General ledger

Sales ledger control account

		£			£
31 Dec 20X8	Balance b/d	7,264	31 Dec 20X8	Irrecoverable debts expense	669
			31 Dec 20X8	Balance c/d	6,595
		7,264			7,264

Irrecoverable debts expense account

		£			£
31 Dec 20X8	Sales ledger control	669	31 Dec 20X8	Bank	488
			31 Dec 20X8	Statement of profit or loss	181
		669			669

Sales ledger

R Trevor

	£		£

BPP LEARNING MEDIA

E Ingham

	£		£
31 Dec 2008 Balance b/d	669	31 Dec 2008 Irrecoverable debts	669

Task 8.4

Sales ledger control account

	£		£
Balance b/d	218,940	Irrecoverable debt expense	2,440
		Balance c/d	216,500
	218,940		218,940

Allowance for doubtful debts account

	£		£
		Balance b/d	5,215
Balance c/d (£216,500 x 3%)	6,495	Allowance for doubtful debts adjustment	1,280
	6,495		6,495

Irrecoverable debts expense account

	£		£
Sales ledger control account	2,440	Statement of profit or loss	2,440

Allowance for doubtful debts adjustment account

	£		£
Allowance for doubtful debts	1,280	Statement of profit or loss	1,280

Task 8.5

✓	
	Accruals
	Consistency
	Materiality
✓	Prudence

Chapter 9

Task 9.1

(a)

Account name	Amount £	Debit (✓)	Credit (✓)
Purchases ledger control account	20	✓	
Bank	20		✓

(b) Bank interest received on the bank statement of £45.

Account name	Amount £	Debit (✓)	Credit (✓)
Bank	45	✓	
Interest received	45		✓

(c) A BACs receipt from a customer for £5,400 has not been entered in the cash book.

Account name	Amount £	Debit (✓)	Credit (✓)
Bank	5,400	✓	
Sales ledger control account	5,400		✓

(d) Cheque number 10810 for £2,356 issued on 29 May, in respect of payment of an invoice for accountancy services, is not showing on the bank statement.

Note for bank reconciliation:

> The cheque should appear as an unpresented cheque in the bank reconciliation. It should be deducted from the balance per the bank statement.

BPP
LEARNING MEDIA

Task 9.2

Adjustment	Amount £	Debit ✓	Credit ✓
1. Bank charges	25	✓	
Bank	25		✓
3. Sales ledger control (£895 – £859)	36		✓
Bank	36	✓	

Notes: For point 2, it is the bank statement that must be corrected, not the cash book. Point 4 relates to an uncredited lodgement which will appear on the bank reconciliation statement.

Task 9.3

Bank reconciliation as at 7 July

	£
Balance per bank statement at 7 July	12,848.66
Add outstanding lodgements	
S Rose	485.21
W Field Suppliers	720.15
R Forge	225.63
Total to add:	1,430.99
Less unpresented cheques	
003124 (still unpaid from previous reconciliation)	589.45
003126	126.89
003127	500.00
003128	896.78
003129	663.14
003130	105.45
003131	4,325.00
Total to subtract:	7,206.71
Balance as per cash book (5,982.91 + 16,372.85 − 15,282.82)	7,072.94

Task 9.4

✓	
	Timing difference
	Bank charges
	Error
✓	Cash receipts total posted to purchases ledger control account

The incorrect posting of the total will not affect the bank reconciliation.

BPP
LEARNING MEDIA

Chapter 10

Task 10.1

Sales ledger control account

	£		£
Balance b/d	4,268	Sales returns	995
Credit sales	15,487	Irrecoverable debt written off	210
Returned cheque	645	Cheques from customers	13,486
		Discounts allowed	408
		Contra	150
		Balance c/d	5,151
	20,400		20,400

Task 10.2

Purchases ledger control account

	£		£
Cheques to suppliers	10,379	Balance b/d	3,299
Returns to suppliers	1,074	Credit purchases	12,376
Discounts received	302		
Contra	230		
Balance c/d	3,690		
	15,675		15,675

Task 10.3

Sales ledger control account

	£		£
Balance b/d	12,634	Cheques from customers	50,375
Credit sales	51,376	Sales returns	3,173
		Contra	630
		Discounts allowed	1,569
		Balance c/d	8,263
	64,010		64,010

Purchases ledger control account

	£		£
Discounts received	1,245	Balance b/d	10,553
Cheques to suppliers	35,795	Credit purchases	40,375
Purchases returns	2,003		
Contra	630		
Balance c/d	11,255		
	50,928		50,928

Task 10.4

Adjustment	Amount £	Debit ✓	Credit ✓
Adjustment for (a)	1,000	✓	
Adjustment for (b)	90	✓	

Task 10.5

Adjustment	Amount £	Debit ✓	Credit ✓
Adjustment for (a)	576	✓	
Adjustment for (b)	169	✓	
Adjustment for (d)	100		✓

BPP LEARNING MEDIA

Task 10.6

Account name	Debit £	Credit £
Sales ledger control		900.00
Sales	900.00	
Sales (1,440.00 × 5/6)	1,200.00	
VAT (1,440.00 × 1/6)	240.00	
Sales ledger control		1,440.00
Sales ledger control		582.45
Being correction of errors in sales ledger control account		
Purchases ledger control		270.00
Purchases	270.00	
Marketing (872.00 × 5/6)	726.67	
VAT (872.00 × 1/6)	145.33	
Purchases ledger control		872.00
Purchases ledger control	582.45	
Being correction of errors in purchases ledger control account		

Task 10.7

✓	
✓	The sales day book has been undercast by £1,000
	Settlement discounts totalling £1,000 have been omitted from the general ledger
	One sales ledger account with a credit balance of £1,000 has been treated as a debit balance
	The cash receipts book has been undercast by £1,000

 BPP LEARNING MEDIA

Explanation

The total of sales invoices in the day book is debited to the control account. If the total is understated by £1,000, the debits in the control account will also be understated by £1,000. Options B and D would have the opposite effect: credit entries in the control account would be understated. Option C would lead to a discrepancy of 2 × £1,000 = £2,000.

Task 10.8

✓	Control account	List of balances
	Debit £45	Add £45
✓	Credit £45	Add £45
	Debit £45	Subtract £45
	Credit £45	Subtract £45

Explanation

This affects both the total which was posted to the control account and the individual posting to the purchases ledger.

Task 10.9

✓	Discounts allowed	Discounts received
	Debit purchases ledger control	Credit sales ledger control
	Credit purchases ledger control	Credit sales ledger control
	Debit sales ledger control	Credit purchases ledger control
✓	Credit sales ledger control	Debit purchases ledger control

Both the amount due from customers and the amount due to suppliers are being reduced by discounts allowed and discounts received respectively.

BPP
LEARNING MEDIA

Chapter 11

Task 11.1

Error	Imbalance ✓	No imbalance ✓
The payment of the telephone bill was posted to the cash payments book and then credited to the telephone account	✓	
The depreciation expense was debited to the accumulated depreciation account and credited to the depreciation expense account		✓
The electricity account balance of £750 was taken to the trial balance as £570	✓	
The motor expenses were debited to the motor vehicles at cost account		✓
The discounts received in the cash payments book were not posted to the general ledger		✓

Task 11.2

£	8,304	Credit balance

Task 11.3

(a)

Account name	Debit £	Credit £
Telephone account	236	
Electricity account		236
Being correction of misposting of telephone expense		

(b)

Account name	Debit £	Credit £
Sales ledger control account	180	
Sales account		180
Being correction of sales invoice entry in the sales day book		

(c)

Account name	Debit £	Credit £
Purchases ledger control account	38	
Purchases returns account		38
Being entry of credit note omitted from purchases returns day book		

(d)

Account name	Debit £	Credit £
Allowance for doubtful debts adjustment account	254	
Allowance for doubtful debts		254
Being correction of error in increasing allowance for doubtful debts		

(e)

Account name	Debit £	Credit £
Purchases ledger control account	400	
Sales ledger control account		400
Being correction of misposting of contra entry		

Task 11.4

Suspense account

	£		£
Sales ledger control	2,700	Balance b/d	1,370
Sales ledger control (£235 × 2)	470	Wages – trial balance	1,800
	3,170		3,170

BPP LEARNING MEDIA

Task 11.5

Suspense account

	£		£
Balance b/d	3,100	Insurance (1,585 × 2)	3,170
Postage (62 – 26)	36		
Bank interest received – TB	34		
	3,170		3,170

Task 11.6

Account name	Debit £	Credit £
Accumulated depreciation	10,500	
Disposal account	15,000	
Suspense	4,000	
Non-current asset at cost		15,000
Disposal account		10,500
Disposal account		4,000

Task 11.7

Account name	Debit £	Credit £
Suspense	1,641.38	
Wages		270.00
Purchases ledger control		180.00
Sales ledger control		1,191.38

BPP
LEARNING MEDIA

Task 11.8

transposition error
error of omission
error of commission
error of principle
reversal of entries

Note: Other examples of errors as set out in Chapter 11 are also acceptable.

Task 11.9

The total of debit balances in the TB therefore | exceeds | the total of credit balances by

£	500

Task 11.10

✓			
	Debit	Discounts received	£350
	Credit	Suspense	£350
	Debit	Suspense	£350
	Credit	Discounts received	£350
	Debit	Discounts received	£700
	Credit	Suspense	£700
✓	Debit	Suspense	£700
	Credit	Discounts received	£700

BPP
LEARNING MEDIA

Task 11.11

	Workings	£
Rent	£3,600 + £1,200	4,800
Insurance	£4,250 – £850	3,400

Task 11.12

Account name		Debit £	Credit £
(i)	Selling expenses	340	
	Bank		340
(ii)	Purchases	360	
	Suspense		360
(iii)	Suspense	690	
	Discount received		690
(iv)	Inventory – SFP	18,200	
	Inventory – SPL		18,200
(v)	Irrecoverable debts expense	2,800	
	Sales ledger control		2,800
	Irrecoverable debts expense	48	
	Allowance for doubtful debts		48
	(£20,200 – 2,800) × 2% – 300		
(vi)	Administration expenses	680	
	Accrued expenses		680
	Being accrued administration expenses		
(vii)	Prepayments of expenses	440	
	Administration expenses		440

Account name		Debit £	Credit £
(viii)	Depreciation expense – machinery (£58,400 × 20%)	11,680	
	Accumulated depreciation – machinery		11,680
	Depreciation expense – motor vehicles (£22,100 – 9,680) × 25%	3,105	
	Accumulated depreciation – motor vehicles		3,105

Task 11.13

✓	
✓	Debit £1,350
	Credit £1,350
	Debit £13,650
	Credit £13,650

Task 11.14

The suspense account shows a debit balance of £100. This could be due to:

✓	
	Entering £50 received from A Turner on the debit side of A Turner's account
	Entering £50 received from A Turner on the credit side of A Turner's account
	Undercasting the sales day book by £100
✓	Undercasting the sales ledger account by £100

The first two options will affect only the personal ledger account of A Turner. The third option will affect both sides of the double entry.

BPP LEARNING MEDIA

Chapter 12

Task 12.1

(a)

	£	Initial trial balance Debit £	Initial trial balance Credit £	Adjustments Debit £	Adjustments Credit £
Accumulated depreciation					
– furniture and fittings	6,100		6,100		2,450
– motor vehicles	22,000		22,000		7,800
Accrued expenses					1,000
Allowance for doubtful debts	1,000		1,000		200
Allowance for doubtful debts adjustment				200	
Bank overdraft	1,650		1,650		
Capital	74,000		74,000		
Depreciation expense – furniture & fittings				2,450	
Depreciation expense – motor vehicles				7,800	
Discounts allowed	2,100	2,100		850	
Discounts received	1,800		1,800		200
Drawings	30,000	30,000			
Electricity	2,300	2,300		650	
Furniture and fittings at cost	24,500	24,500			
Insurance	3,000	3,000			700
Irrecoverable debts expense				1,500	
Miscellaneous expenses	1,200	1,200		300	
Motor expenses	3,400	3,400			300
Motor vehicles at cost	48,000	48,000			
Prepayments				1,500	

		Initial trial balance		Adjustments	
	£	Debit £	Credit £	Debit £	Credit £
Purchases	245,000	245,000			
Purchases ledger control	40,800		40,800		
Rent paid	4,200	4,200			800
Sales	369,000		369,000		
Sales ledger control	61,500	61,500			1,500
Inventory	41,000	41,000		43,500	43,500
Suspense			650	200	850
Telephone	1,600	1,600		350	
VAT due to HMRC	4,100		4,100		
Wages	52,000	52,000			
		520,450	520,450	59,300	59,300

(b)

Account name	Debit £	Credit £
Inventory – statement of financial position	43,500	
Inventory – statement of profit or loss		43,500
Depreciation expense – furniture and fittings (£24,500 × 10%)	2,450	
Accumulated depreciation – furniture and fittings		2,450
Depreciation expense – motor vehicles ((£48,000 – £22,000) × 30%)	7,800	
Accumulated depreciation – motor vehicles		7,800
Irrecoverable debts expense	1,500	
Sales ledger control account		1,500
Allowance for doubtful debts adjustment (((£61,500 – £1,500) × 2%) – £1,000)	200	
Allowance for doubtful debts		200
Electricity	650	

Account name	Debit £	Credit £
Telephone	350	
Accrued expenses		1,000
Prepayments	1,500	
Rent		800
Insurance (£1,200 × 7/12)		700

(c)

Account name	Debit £	Credit £
Miscellaneous expenses	300	
Motor expenses		300
Discounts allowed (£425 × 2)	850	
Suspense		850
Suspense	200	
Discounts received (£100 × 2)		200

Task 12.2

Workings

Depreciation on motor vehicles: £(23,800 − 12,140) × 30% = £3,498

Depreciation on computer: £2,400 × 25% = £600

Depreciation on furniture and fittings: £12,800 × 20% = £2,560

Answer bank

Account name	Ledger balance Debit £	Ledger balance Credit £	Adjustments Debit £	Adjustments Credit £	SPL Debit £	SPL Credit £	SFP Debit £	SFP Credit £
Inventory at 1 June 20X7	1,600		2,100	2,100	1,600	2,100	2,100	
Motor vehicles at cost	23,800						23,800	
Computer at cost	2,400						2,400	
Furniture and fittings at cost	12,800						12,800	
Accumulated depreciation at 1 June 20X7:								
Motor vehicles		12,140		3,498				15,638
Computer		600		600				1,200
Furniture and fittings		2,560		2,560				5,120
Wages	16,400				16,400			
Telephone	900				900			
Electricity	1,200		400		1,600			
Advertising	400		100		500			
Stationery	600			100	500			
Motor expenses	1,700				1,700			
Miscellaneous expenses	300				300			
Insurance	1,000			300	700			
Sales		86,400				86,400		
Purchases	38,200				38,200			
Sales ledger control	7,200						7,200	
Allowance for doubtful debts at 1 June 20X7		200		88				288
Bank (debit balance)	1,300						1,300	
Petty cash	100						100	
Purchases ledger control		3,180						3,180

BPP
LEARNING MEDIA

Account name	Ledger balance		Adjustments		SPL		SFP	
	Debit £	Credit £	Debit £	Credit £	Debit £	Credit £	Debit £	Credit £
VAT (credit balance)		940						960
Capital		25,000						25,000
Drawings	21,140						21,140	
Depreciation expense:								
Motor vehicles			3,498		3,498			
Computer			600		600			
Furniture and fittings			2,560		2,560			
Accruals				400				400
Prepayments			300				300	
Allowance for doubtful debts adjustment			88		88			
Profit / loss					19,354			19,354
	131,040	131,040	9,646	9,646	88,500	88,500	71,140	71,140

Task 12.3

Workings

Depreciation on machinery: £(68,000 − 34,680) × 30% = £9,996
Depreciation on furniture and fittings: £32,400 × 20% = £6,480

Ledger account	Ledger balances		Adjustments		Statement of profit or loss		Statement of financial position	
	Dr £	Cr £	Dr £	Cr £	Dr £	Cr £	Dr £	Cr £
Capital		150,000						150,000
Purchases ledger control		40,400						40,400
Sales ledger control	114,500			1,500			113,000	
Sales		687,000				687,000		
Inventory at 1 July 20X7	40,400				40,400			
Closing inventory			42,800	42,800		42,800	42,800	
Machinery at cost	68,000						68,000	
Furniture and fittings at cost	32,400						32,400	
Wages	98,700				98,700			
Sales returns	4,800			360	4,440			
Telephone	4,100		400		4,500			
Purchases	485,000				485,000			
Heat and light	3,400		1,010		4,410			
Advertising	8,200				8,200			
Purchases returns		3,000				3,000		
Selling costs	9,400				9,400			
Discounts received		4,700		450		5,150		
Discounts allowed	3,900				3,900			
Administrative expenses	14,800			700	14,100			
Miscellaneous expenses	400				400			
Accumulated depreciation at 1 July 20X7:								
Machinery		34,680		9,996				44,676
Furniture and fittings		6,480		6,480				12,960
Allowance for doubtful debts at 1 July 20X7		2,000		260				2,260

BPP LEARNING MEDIA

Ledger account	Ledger balances		Adjustments		Statement of profit or loss		Statement of financial position	
	Dr £	Cr £	Dr £	Cr £	Dr £	Cr £	Dr £	Cr £
Drawings	36,860						36,860	
Bank (debit balance)	6,400						6,400	
VAT (credit balance)		3,200						3,200
Suspense account (debit balance)	200		450 360	1,010				
Depreciation expenses:								
Machinery			9,996		9,996			
Furniture and fittings			6,480		6,480			
Irrecoverable debt expense			1,500		1,500			
Allowance for doubtful debts adjustment			260		260			
Accruals				400				400
Prepayments			700				700	
Profit					46,264			46,264
	931,460	931,460	63,956	63,956	737,950	737,950	300,160	300,160

Task 12.4

Account name	Trial balance Debit £	Trial balance Credit £	Adjustments Debit £	Adjustments Credit £	SPL Debit £	SPL Credit £	SFP Debit £	SFP Credit £
Administration costs	72,019.27		480.00	320.00	72,179.27			
Bank overdraft		8,290.12						8,290.12
Capital		50,000.00		10,000.00				60,000.00
Loan		100,000.00						100,000.00
Depreciation charge	12,000.00		16,000.00		28,000.00			
Drawings	36,000.00						36,000.00	
Non-current assets: Cost	120,287.00		4,000.00				124,287.00	
Non-current assets: Depreciation		36,209.28		1,000.00				37,209.28
Interest: paid	12,182.26		650.00		12,832.26			
Interest: received		21.00				21.00		
Wages	167,302.39		14,248.40		181,550.79			
Raw materials	104,293.38				104,293.38			
Inventory as at 1/6/X7	25,298.30				25,298.30			
Purchases ledger control		42,190.85						42,190.85
Sales		481,182.20				481,182.20		
Sales ledger control	156,293.00			6,092.35			150,200.65	
Suspense	17,156.05		6,092.35 10,000.00	15,000.00 14,248.40 4,000.00				
VAT payable		4,938.20						4,938.20
Accruals				480.00 650.00				1,130.00
Prepayments			320.00				320.00	
Closing inventory			32,125.28	32,125.28		32,125.28	32,125.28	
Profit					89,174.48			89,174.48
	722,831.65	722,831.65	83,916.03	83,916.03	513,328.48	513,328.48	342,932.93	342,932.93

BPP LEARNING MEDIA

Task 12.5

When an extended trial balance is extended and a business has made a profit, this figure for profit will be in the [debit] column of the statement of profit or loss.

Task 12.6

What is the double entry to record closing inventory on the ETB?

	Account name
Debit	Inventory – statement of financial position
Credit	Inventory – statement of profit or loss

Task 12.7

Which of these statements is/are correct?

(i) A casting error in a day book will stop the trial balance balancing.
(ii) A transposition error in a daybook will stop the trial balance balancing.

✓	
	(i) only
	(i) and (ii)
	(ii) only
✓	Neither (i) or (ii)

Task 12.8

✓	Debit £450
	Credit £450
	Debit £4,550
	Credit £4,550

Working

Suspense account

	£		£
Balance b/d	450		
Discounts received	2,050	Discounts allowed	2,500
	2,500		2,500

BPP
LEARNING MEDIA

AAT AQ2013 SAMPLE ASSESSMENT 1
ACCOUNTS PREPARATION

Time allowed: 2 hours

Task 1 (18 marks)

This task is about the non-current assets register for a business known as AMBR Trading. AMBR Trading has a financial year end of 31 March.

The following is a purchase invoice received by AMBR Trading relating to some items to be used in its office:

To: AMBR Trading Unit 6, East End Trading Estate Southgrove HS14 6PW	Refurb & Co 82 Maryland Street Bishops Moat SH34 9TT		Date: 24 June 20X6 Invoice RE2391
Item	Details	Quantity	£
Refurbished operator chairs	3 × Ergo 803 and 3 × Ergo 697 @ £60 each	6	360.00
Oak boardroom table	2 metres × 1 metre	1	850.00
Delivery and assembly of oak table		1	75.00
Oak maintenance and repair kit		1	60.00
Total			1,345.00
Delivery date: 24/06/X6			

AMBR paid the invoice in full on 31 July 20X6 using a £1,345.00 bank loan.

This amount is to be repaid over 12 months.

The following information relates to the sale of a motor vehicle no longer required by the business:

Description	1.6 litre car – AF05 LKR
Date of sale	23 September 20X6
Selling price	£5,340.00

- VAT can be ignored.
- AMBR Trading has a policy of capitalising expenditure over £350.
- Furniture and fittings are depreciated at 15% per year on a straight-line basis assuming no residual value.
- Motor vehicles are depreciated at 25% per year on a diminishing balance basis.
- A full year's depreciation is applied in the year of acquisition and none in the year of disposal.

Complete the extract from the non-current assets register below for:

(a) **Any acquisitions of non-current assets during the year ended 31 March 20X7.**
(b) **Any disposals of non-current assets during the year ended 31 March 20X7.**
(c) **Depreciation for the year ended 31 March 20X7.**

Note. Not every cell will require an entry, and not all cells will accept entries.
Show your answers to 2 decimal places.

Extract from non-current assets register

Description/ Serial number	Acquisition date	Cost £	Depreciation charges £	Carrying amount £	Funding method	Disposal proceeds £	Disposal date
Furniture and fittings							
Filling racks	31/10/X5	832.60			Cash		
Year end 31/03/X6			124.89	707.71			
Year end 31/03/X7							
▽					▽		
Year end 31/03/X7							
Motor vehicles							
1.6 litre car AF05 LKR	01/09/X4	10,600.00			Part-exchange and cash		
Year end 31/03/X5			2,650.00	7,950.00			
Year end 31/03/X6			1,987.50	5,962.50			
Year end 31/03/X7			▽	▽			
1.8 litre van AD05 ACT	01/09/X5	10,400.00			Part-exchange and cash		
Year end 31/03/X5			2,600.00	7,800.00			
Year end 31/03/X6			1,950.00	5,850.00			
Year end 31/03/X7							

BPP LEARNING MEDIA

Drop-down list:

1.6 litre car AF05 LKR
1.8 litre van AD05 ACT
Boardroom table and chairs
Oak boardroom table
Cash
Part-exchange and cash
Loan
1,987.50
1,490.63
496.88
0.00
5,465.62
4,471.87
3,975.00
0.00

....

Task 2 (17 marks)

This task is about ledger accounting for non-current assets.

You are working on the accounting records of a business for the year ended 31 March 20X7.

- VAT can be ignored.

- An item of computer equipment was part-exchanged on 1 October 20X6.

- The original item was bought for £3,690 on 14 August 20X4.

- Depreciation is provided at one third of original cost per year on a straight line basis.

- A full year's depreciation is applied in the year of acquisition and none in the year of disposal.

- A part-exchange allowance of £1,350 was given.

- £3,480 was paid from the bank to complete the purchase of the new equipment.

Make entries relating to the disposal.

(a) **Complete the disposals account.**

   Update the bank account.

On each account, show clearly the balance to be carried down or transferred to the statement of profit or loss, as appropriate.

Disposals

	£		£
vehicle at cost ▼	3690	Accumulated ▼	2460
Bank ▼	3480	comuter equip at cost ▼	1350
SPL ▼	120	▼	
▼		▼	

Bank

	£		£
Balance b/d	10,340	Computer ▼	3480
▼		c/d ▼	6860
▼		▼	
	10 340		10 340

Drop-down list:

Balance b/d
Balance c/d
Bank
Computer consumables
Computer equipment accumulated depreciation
Computer equipment at cost
Depreciation charges
Disposals
Profit or loss account
Purchases
Purchases ledger control account
Sales
Sales ledger control account

(b) **Calculate the purchase cost of the new computer equipment from the information above.**

£ _____

The computer room has been rewired to accommodate the new computer equipment. The work was done by employees of the business. On the same day, the air conditioning in the computer room was repaired by outside contractors. The cost were as follows:

- Wages to rewire computer room: £220
- Materials to rewire computer room: £430
- Computer room air conditioning repair: £170

(c) **What is the additional cost to be recorded as capital expenditure? Choose ONE answer.**

Nil ☐

£430 ☐

£650 600 ☑

£820 ☐

Task 3 (16 marks)

This task is about accounting for accruals and prepayments of income and expenses.

You are working on the accounting records of a business for the year ended 31 March 20X7. In this task, you can ignore VAT.

You have the following information:

- The balance on the commission receivable account at the beginning of the financial year is £2,400. This represents an accrual for commission receivable as the end of the year on 31 March 20X6.

- The cashbook for the year shows **receipts** for commission receivable of £29,150.

- The commission receivable account has been correctly adjusted for £1,800 commission for the quarter ended 31 March 20X7. This was received into the bank and entered into the cashbook on 21 April 20X7.

- Double entry accounting is done in the general ledger.

(a) **Complete the following statements:**

On 01/01/X6, the commission receivable account shows a [▼] balance of £[ ].

On 31/03/X7, the commission receivable account shows an adjustment for [▼] of £[ ].

Drop-down list:

Credit
Debit
Accrued expenses
Accrued income
Prepaid expenses
Prepaid income

(b) **Calculate the commission receivable for the year ended 31/03/X7.**

£ [   ]

The cashbook for the year shows payments for administration expenses of £12,580.

(c) **Update the administration expenses account for this, showing clearly the balance to be carried down.**

Administration expenses

	£		£
▼		Accrued expenses b/d	1,990
▼		▼	
▼		▼	

Drop-down list:

Accrued expenses
Accrued income
Administration expenses
Balance b/d
Balance c/d
Bank
Commission receivable
Prepaid expenses
Prepaid income
Purchases
Purchases ledger control account
Sales
Sales ledger control account
Statement of financial position

You now find out that there is an unpaid bill of £1,185 for secretarial services for the three months ended 30 April 20X7 that has not been included in the accounting records. Secretarial services are classified under administration expenses.

(d) **Taking into account this information, complete the following statements:**

The amount to be transferred to the statement of profit or loss for administration expenses will be £ [   ] [▼] than the figure carried down in (c).

Administration expenses will show as a [▼] in the profit or loss account in the general ledger.

Drop-down list:

Greater
Less
Debit
Credit

. . . .

Task 4 (19 marks)

This task is about preparing a trial balance and reconciliations.

You are working on the accounting records of a business with a year end of 31 March.

You have five extracts from the ledger accounts as at 31 March 20X7:

Bank

		£		£
31/03/X7	Balance b/f	8,103		

Internet and telephone costs

		£		£
31/03/X7	Balance b/f	1,480		

This balance has been adjusted for prepaid expenses of £135 as at 31/03/X7.

Irrecoverable debts

	£			£
		31/03/X7	Balance b/f	230

VAT

	£			£
		31/03/X7	Balance b/f	4,296

Vending machine income

	£			£
		31/03/X7	Balance b/f	2,010

This balance has been adjusted for accrued income for £170 as at 31/03/X7.

BPP
LEARNING MEDIA

There were no accruals or prepayments of expenses and income other than those stated.

You need to start preparing the initial trial balance as at 31 March 20X7.

(a) **Using all the information given above and the figures given in the table below, enter amounts in the appropriate trial balance columns for the accounts shown.**

Do NOT enter zeros in unused column cells. Do NOT enter any figures as negatives.

Extract from the trial balance as at 31 March 20X7:

Account	Ledger balance £	Trial balance £ Dr	£ Cr
Accrued income			
Bank			
Drawings	26,000		
Internet and telephone costs			
Irrecoverable debts			
Loan interest received	50		
Loan receivable	2,000		
Prepaid expenses			
VAT			
Vending machine income			

You are now ready to prepare the bank reconciliation.

The balance showing on the bank statement is a credit of £7,162 and the balance in the cashbook is a debit of £8,103.

The bank statement has been compared with the cashbook and the following differences identified:

1. Bank interest received of £68 has not been entered in the cashbook.

2. Cash sales receipts totalling £260 have been entered into the cashbook but are not yet banked.

3. A direct debit payment of £427 has been recorded in the accounting records as £400.

4. An automated payment to a suppliers of £710 has been delayed by the bank due to an error in the account number given.

5. A BACS receipt of £1,090 from a customer has been entered in the cashbook but is not yet showing on the bank statement.

6. A cheque from a customer for £3,850 has been dishonoured by the bank. When adjusting the accounting records, an incorrect amount of £3,508 was entered.

(b) **Use the following table to show the THREE adjustments you need to make to the cashbook.**

Adjustment		Amount £	Debit	Credit
	▼			
	▼			
	▼			

Drop-down list:

Adjustment for (1)
Adjustment for (2)
Adjustment for (3)
Adjustment for (4)
Adjustment for (5)
Adjustment for (6)

Task 5 (20 marks)

This task is about accounting adjustments and journals.

You are working on the accounting records of a business with a year end of 31 March. A trial balance has been drawn up and a suspense account opened. You now need to make some corrections and adjustments for the year ended 31 March 20X7.

You may ignore VAT in this task.

Record the journal entries needed in the general ledger to deal with the items below.

You should:

- **Remove any incorrect entries where appropriate**
- **Post the correct entries.**

You do not need to give narratives.

Do NOT enter zeros into unused column cells.

(a) Travel expenses of £620 have been posted to the vehicle at cost account in error. The other side of the entry is correct.

Journal

	Dr £	Cr £
▼		
▼		

(b) Office repairs costing £84 were paid for using cash. Only the credit side of the double entry was made.

Journal

	Dr £	Cr £
▼		
▼		

(c) No entries have been made for closing inventory as at 31 March 20X7. It has been valued at sales price of £17,820. The sales price of goods is always 20% higher than the cost of those goods.

Journal

	Dr £	Cr £
▼		
▼		

(d) Discounts allowed of £2,290 have been posted on both sides of the double entry as £2,920.

Journal

	Dr £	Cr £
▼		
▼		
▼		
▼		

BPP LEARNING MEDIA

Drop-down list:

Allowance for doubtful debts
Allowance for doubtful debts adjustment
Bank
Cash
Closing inventory – statement of financial position
Closing inventory – statement of profit or loss
Depreciation charges
Discounts allowed
Discounts received
Irrecoverable debts
Office furniture accumulated depreciation
Office furniture at cost
Purchases
Purchases ledger control account
Purchases returns
Repairs and maintenance
Sales
Sales ledger control account
Suspense
Travel expenses
Vehicles accumulated depreciation
Vehicles at costs

Task 6 (20 marks)

This task is about the extended trial balance and showing your knowledge of good accounting practice.

You have the following extended trial balance. The adjustments have already been correctly entered.

(a) **Extend the figures into the statement of profit or loss (SPL) and statement of financial position (SFP) columns.**

Do NOT enter zeros into unused column cells.

Complete the extended trial balance by entering figures and a label in the correct places.

Extended trial balance

Ledger account	Ledger balances		Adjustments		Statement of profit or loss		Statement of financial position	
	Dr £	Cr £	Dr £	Cr £	Dr £	Cr £	Dr £	Cr £
Bank		1,326		380				
Capital		14,600						
Closing inventory			13,740	13,740				
Depreciation charges	5,200							
Equipment at cost	26,950			950				
Equipment accumulated depreciation		20,800						
General expenses	30,870		950	400				
Interest paid	370		380					
Loan		8,500	1,500					
Opening inventory	18,590							
Prepayments			400					
Purchases	109,970							
Purchases ledger control account		18,740						
Sales		174,760		670				
Sales ledger control account	23,500							
Suspense	830		670	1,500				
VAT		1,554						
Wages	24,000							
▼								
TOTAL	240,280	240,280	17,640	17,640				

Drop-down list:

Gross profit/loss for the year
Profit/loss for the year
Balance c/d
Suspense
Balance b/d

A trainee at your workplace has asked you for help in understanding accounting concepts.

(b) **Of the following, which ONE provides the best example of an application of the accruals concept?**

Valuing inventory at the lower of cost and net realisable value. ☐

Classifying an item of low cost as revenue rather than capital expenditure, even though it has a life of more than one year. ☐

Writing off an irrecoverable debt after a customer has gone out of business. ☐

Writing of the cost of a non-current asset by using depreciation. ☐

(c) **Which ONE of the following would you expect to find in the general ledger?**

Drag and drop the correct item into the space below.

Found in the general ledger

Sales ledger control account

Sales day-book

Individual customer account

Sales order book

You are working on the accounting records of a business whose entire inventory was destroyed by fire in the last week of the financial year.

Since the year end, the trader's insurance claim for the full value of the destroyed inventory has been settled.

The accountant has told you that the value of this insurance claim will be treated as a current asset in the year-end financial statements.

(d) **Which of the following describes why the value of the insurance claim is a current asset? Choose ONE.**

It is a sum payable by the business in the short term. ☐

It represents items which are each to be used in the business over more than one accounting period. ☐

It is an amount receivable by the business. ☐

It is an amount payable by the business that is due more than a year after the year-end date. ☐

BPP
LEARNING MEDIA

AAT AQ2013 SAMPLE ASSESSMENT 1
ACCOUNTS PREPARATION

ANSWERS

Task 1 (18 marks)

Description/ Serial number	Acquisition Date	Cost £	Depreciation charges £	Carrying amount £	Funding method	Disposal proceeds £	Disposal date
Furniture and fittings							
Filing racks	31/10/X5	832.60			Cash		
Year end 31/03/X6			124.89	707.71			
Year end 31/03/X7			124.89	582.82			
Oak boardroom table ▼	24/06/X6	925			Loan ▼		
Year end 31/03/X7			138.75	786.25			
Motor vehicles							
1.6 litre car AF05 LKR	01/09/X4	10,600.00			Part-exchange and cash		
Year end 31/03/X5			2,650.00	7,950.00			
Year end 31/03/X6			1,987.50	5,962.50			
Year end 31/03/X7			0.00 ▼	0.00 ▼		5,340	23/09/X6
1.8 litre van AD05 ACT	01/03/X5	10,400.00			Part-exchange and cash		
Year end 31/03/X5			2,600.00	7,800.00			
Year end 31/03/X6			1,950.00	5,850.00			
Year end 31/03/X7			1,462.50	4,387.50			

Task 2 (17 marks)

(a)

Disposals

	£		£
Computer equipment at cost ▼	3,690	Computer equipment accumulated depreciation ▼	2,460
Profit or loss account ▼	120	Computer equipment at cost ▼	1,350
▼		▼	
▼		▼	
	3,810		3,810

Bank

	£		£
Balance b/d	10,340	Computer equipment at cost ▼	3,480
▼		Balance c/d ▼	6,860
▼		▼	
	10,340		10,340

(b) **Calculate the purchase cost of the new computer equipment from the information above.**

£ | 4,830 |

The computer room has been rewired to accommodate the new computer equipment. The work was done by employees of the business. On the same day, the air conditioning in the computer room was repaired by outside contractors. The costs were as follows:

- Wages to rewire computer room: £220
- Materials to rewire computer room: £430
- Computer room air conditioning repair: £170

(c) **What is the additional cost to he recorded as capital expenditure? Choose ONE answer.**

Nil	☐
£430	☐
£650	☑
£820	☐

BPP LEARNING MEDIA

Task 3 (16 marks)

(a) **Complete the following statements:**

On 01/04/X6, the commission receivable account shows a | debit ▼ |
balance of £ | 2,400 |

On 31/03/X7, the commission receivable account shows an adjustment for:

| accrued income ▼ | of £ | 1,800 |

(b) **Calculate the commission receivable for the year ended 31/03/37.**

£ | 28,550 |

The cashbook for the year shows payments for administration expenses of £12,580.

(c) **Update the administration expenses account for this, showing clearly the balance to be carried down.**

Administration expenses

		£			£
Bank	▼	12,580	Accrued expenses b/d		1,990
	▼		Balance c/d	▼	10,590
	▼			▼	
		12,580			12,580

You now find out that there is an unpaid bill of £1,185 for secretarial services for the three months ended 30 April 20X7 that has not been included in the accounting records. Secretarial services are classified under administration expenses.

(d) **Taking into account this information, complete the following statements:**

The amount to be transferred to the statement of profit or loss for administration expenses will be £ | 790 | | greater ▼ | than the figure carried down in (c).

Administration expenses will show as a | debit ▼ | in the statement of profit or loss account in the general ledger.

Task 4 (19 marks)

(a) **Using all the information given above and the figures given in the table below, enter amounts in the appropriate trial balance columns for the accounts shown.**

Do NOT enter zeros in unused column cells. Do NOT enter any figures as negatives.

Extract from the trial balance as at 31 March 20X7:

Account	Ledger £	Trial balance £ Dr	Trial balance £ Cr
Accrued income		170	
Bank		8,103	
Drawings	26,000	26,000	
Internet and telephone cost		1,480	
Irrecoverable debts			230
Loan interest received	50		50
Loan receivable	2,000	2,000	
Prepaid expenses		135	
VAT			4,296
Vending machine income			2,010

(b) **Use the following table to show the THREE adjustments you need to make to the cashbook.**

Adjustment	Amount £	Debit	Credit
Adjustment for (1) ▼	68	✓	
Adjustment for (3) ▼	27		✓
Adjustment for (6) ▼	342		✓

BPP LEARNING MEDIA

Task 5 (20 marks)

(a) Travel expenses of £620 have been posted to the vehicles at cost account in error. The other side of the entry is correct.

Journal

		Dr £	Cr £
Travel expenses	▼	620	
Vehicle at cost	▼		620

(b) Office repairs costing £84 were paid for using cash. Only the credit side of the double entry was made.

Journal

		Dr £	Cr £
Repairs and maintenance	▼	84	
Suspense	▼		84

(c) No entries have been made for closing inventory as at 31 March 20X7. It has been valued at sales price of £17,820. The sales price of goods is always 20% higher than the cost of those goods.

Journal

		Dr £	Cr £
Closing inventory – statement of financial position	▼	14,850	
Closing inventory – statement of profit or loss	▼		14,850

(d) Discounts allowed of £2,290 have been posted on both sides of the double entry as £2,920.

Journal

		Dr £	Cr £
Sales ledger control account	▼	2,920	
Discounts allowed	▼		2,920
Sales ledger control account	▼		2,290
Discounts allowed	▼	2,290	

Task 6 (20 marks)

(a) Extended trial balance

Ledger account	Ledger balances		Adjustments		Statement of profit of loss		Statement of financial position	
	Dr £	Cr £	Dr £	Cr £	Dr £	Cr £	Dr £	Cr £
Bank		1,326		380				1,706
Capital		14,600						14,600
Closing inventory			13,740	13,740		13,740	13,740	
Depreciation charges	5,200				5,200			
Equipment at cost	26,950			950			26,000	
Equipment accumulated depreciation		20,800						20,800
General expenses	30,870		950	400	31,420			
Interest paid	370		380		750			
Loan		8,500	1,500					7,000
Opening inventory	18,590				18,590			
Prepayments			400				400	
Purchases	109,970				109,970			
Purchases ledger control account		18,740						18,740
Sales		174,760		670		175,430		
Sales ledger control account	23,500						23,500	
Suspense	830		670	1,500				
VAT		1,554						1,554
Wages	24,000				24,000			
Profit/loss for the year ▼						760	760	
TOTAL	240,280	240,280	17,640	17,640	189,930	189,930	64,400	64,400

BPP  LEARNING MEDIA

(b) **Of the following, which ONE provides the best example of an application of the accruals concept?**

Valuing inventory at the lower of cost and net realisable value. ☐

Classifying an item of low cost as revenue rather than capital expenditure, even though it has a life of more than one year. ☐

Writing off an irrecoverable debt after a customer has gone out of business. ☐

Writing off the cost of non-current asset by using depreciation. ☑

(c) **Which ONE of the following would you expect to find in the general ledger?**

Drag and drop the correct item into the space below.

Found in the general ledger

	Sales ledger control account
Sales day-book	
Individual customer account	
Sales order hook	

(d) **Which of the following describes why the value of the insurance claim is a current assets? Choose ONE.**

It is a sum payable by the business in the short term. ☐

It represents items which are each to be used in the business over more than one accounting period. ☐

It is an amount receivable by the business. ☑

It is an amount payable by the business that is clue more than a year after the year-end date. ☐

AAT AQ2013 SAMPLE ASSESSMENT 2
ACCOUNTS PREPARATION

Time allowed: 2 hours

BPP
LEARNING MEDIA

Task 1

This task is about the non-current assets register for a business known as AMBR Trading. AMBR Trading is registered for VAT and has a financial year end of 31 March.

The following is a purchase invoice received by AMBR Trading relating to some items to be used in its factory:

To: AMBR Trading Unit 6, East End Trading Estate Southgrove HS14 6PW	PM Trading Ltd Watchet Way Marston BT23 4RR		Date: 01 April X6 Invoice 23953 VAT 203 9613 01GB
			£
Power lathe PM892	Delivery 01 April X6	1	9,930.00
Maintenance contract – 24 months	01/04/X6 – 31/03/X8	1	625.00
Testing – customer premises	2 hrs @ £129.90	2	259.80
Net total			10,814.80
VAT @ 20%			2,162.96
Total			12,977.76
This invoice is to be settled by a hire-purchase agreement. 10% deposit is due on the delivery date.			

The following information relates to the sale of an item of office equipment no longer needed by the business:

Item description	Reception desk – FaradyR
Date of sale	30 September 20X6
Selling price excluding VAT	£600.00

- AMBR Trading has a policy of capitalising expenditure over £1,000.

- Machinery is depreciated at 25% per year on a diminishing balance basis.

- Office equipment is depreciated over eight years on a straight line basis assuming no residual value.

- Depreciation is calculated on an annual basis and charged in equal instalments for each full month an asset is owned in the year.

Complete the extract from the non-current assets register below for:

(a) **Any acquisitions of non-current assets during the year ended 31 March 20X7**
(b) **Any disposals of non-current assets during the year ended 31 March 20X7**
(c) **Depreciation for the year ended 31 March 20X7.**

Note. Not every cell will require an entry, and not all cells will accept entries.
Show your answers to TWO decimal places.

Extract from non-current assets register

Description/ Serial Number	Acquisition Date	Cost £	Depreciation charges £	Carrying amount £	Funding method	Disposal Proceeds £	Dispos date
Office equipment							
Copier 4	01/04/X5	3,200.00			Finance lease		
Year end 31/03/X6			400.00	2,800.00			
Year end 31/03/X7			400.00				
Reception desk – FaradyR	01/01/X5	1,200.00			Cash		
Year end 31/03/X5			37.50	1,162.50			
Year end 31/03/X6			150.00	1,012.50			
Year end 31/03/X7			▼	▼			
Machinery							
CNC machine CNC3491	01/04/X4	16,400.00			Part-exchange		
Year end 31/03/X5			4,100.00	12,300.00			
Year end 31/03/X6			3,075.00	9,225.00			
Year end 31/03/X7							
	▼					▼	
Year end 31/03/X7							

Drop-down list 1:
150.00
112.50
75.00
Nil

Drop-down list 2:
937.50
900.00
862.50
Nil

Drop-down list 3:
CNC Machine CNC 3491
Power lathe PM892
Reception desk – FaradyR
Copier 4

Drop-down list 4:
Cash
Hire purchase
Part-exchange

BPP LEARNING MEDIA

Task 2

This task is about ledger accounting for non-current assets.

- You are working on the accounting records of a business that is registered for VAT.
- The financial year end is 31 March 20X7.
- A new machine has been acquired.
- The cost excluding VAT was £9,300; this was paid from the bank.
- The residual value is expected to be £1,400 excluding VAT. It is estimated it will be used for four years.
- Machinery is depreciated on a straight line basis. A full year's depreciation is applied in the year of acquisition.
- Depreciation has already been entered into the accounting records for existing machinery.

(a) **Calculate the depreciation charge for the year on the new machine.**

£ [ ]

Make entries to account for:

(b) **The purchase of the new machine.**

(c) **The depreciation charge on the new machine.**

On each account, show clearly the balance to be carried down or transferred to the statement of profit or loss, as appropriate.

Machinery at cost

	£		£
Balance b/d	42,800	▼	
▼		▼	
▼		▼	

Depreciation charges

	£		£
Balance b/d	9,630	▼	
▼		▼	
▼		▼	

Machinery accumulated depreciation

	£		£
▼		Balance b/d	19,260
▼		▼	
▼		▼	

Drop-down list:

Balance b/d
Balance c/d
Bank
Depreciation charges
Disposals
Machinery accumulated depreciation
Machinery at cost
Profit or loss account
Purchases
Purchases ledger control account
Repairs and maintenance
Sales
Sales ledger control account

An item of computer equipment originally purchased for £2,700 and with a carrying amount of £675 has been sold. The loss on disposal was £150. A cheque for the proceeds was banked.

(d) **How much did the business receive for the computer equipment? Ignore VAT.**

£ [   ]

(e) **Which ONE of the following is the main purpose of a non-current asset register?**

To provide internal control. ☐

To provide the selling price of a particular item at the time of its disposal. ☐

To provide a measure of financial performance. ☐

BPP LEARNING MEDIA

Task 3

This task is about accounting for accruals and prepayments of income and expenses.

You are working on the accounting records of a business for the year ended 31 March 20X7. In this task, you can ignore VAT.

You have the following information:

- The balance on the general expenses account at the beginning of the financial year is £2,100.

- This represents an amount paid in advance for insurance.

- The cash book for the year shows payments for general expenses of £12,800.

- The general expenses account has been adjusted for a bill of £1,350 received after the year end for general expenses relating to the month of March 20X7.

- Double entry accounting is done in the general ledger.

(a) **Show how the general ledger account for general expenses looked at the beginning of the financial year. Insert ONE date, ONE description and ONE amount into the correct position in the ledger account.**

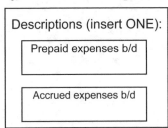

Dates (insert ONE):		Descriptions (insert ONE):	Amounts (insert ONE):	
01/04/X6	01/04/X7	Prepaid expenses b/d	1,350	2,100
31/03/X6	31/03/X7	Accrued expenses b/d		

General expenses

Date	Description	Dr £	Date	Description	Cr £

(b) **Complete the following statement:**

On 31/03/X7, the general expenses account shows a [▼] entry for [▼] carried down of £ [   ] .

Drop-down list 1:   **Drop-down list 2:**

Credit   Accrued expenses
Debit   Prepaid expenses

(c) **Calculate the general expenses for the year ended 31/03/X7.**

£ [   ]

The cash book for the year shows payments for vehicle running expenses of £23,700.

(d) **Update the vehicle running expenses account for this, showing clearly the balance to be carried down.**

Vehicle running expenses

	£			£
▼		Accrued expenses b/d		1,970
▼			▼	
▼			▼	

Drop-down list:

Accrued expenses
Accrued income
Balance b/d
Balance c/d
Bank
General expenses
Prepaid expenses
Prepaid income
Purchases
Purchases ledger control account
Sales
Sales ledger control account
Statement of financial position
Vehicle running expenses

You now find out that the cash book figure for vehicle running expenses includes £375 relating to the period 01/02/X7 to 30/04/X7.

(e) **Taking into account this information, complete the following statement:**

The amount to be transferred to the statement of profit or loss for vehicle running expenses will be £ [   ] [▼] than the figure carried down in (d).

Drop-down list:

Greater
Less

BPP
LEARNING MEDIA

Task 4

This task is about preparing a trial balance and reconciliations.

You are working on the accounting records of a business with a year end of 31 March. You have five extracts from the ledger accounts as at 31 March 20X7. You need to start preparing the trial balance as at 31 March 20X7.

Allowance for doubtful debts adjustment

	£			£
		31/03/X7	Balance b/f	80

Disposal of non-current assets

		£		£
31/03/X7	Balance b/f	780		

Insurance costs

		£		£
31/03/X7	Balance b/f	1,625		

Loan

		£		£
31/03/X7	Balance b/f	1,000		

Miscellaneous income

	£			£
		31/03/X7	Balance b/f	2,537

This balance needs to be adjusted for a prepayment of insurance costs of £325 as at 31/03/X7.

There were no accruals or prepayments of expenses and income other than those stated.

(a) **Using all the information given above and the figures given in the table below, enter amounts in the appropriate trial balance columns for the accounts shown.**

Do NOT enter zeros in unused column cells. Do NOT enter any figures as negatives.

Extract from the trial balance as at 31 March 20X7	Ledger balance	Trial balance	
Account	£	£ Dr	£ Cr
Allowance for doubtful debts adjustment			
Capital	30,000		
Disposal of non-current assets			
Insurance costs			
Loan			
Loan interest received	50		
Miscellaneous income			
Payroll expenses	9,600		
Prepaid expenses			

You are now ready to prepare the reconciliation of the purchases ledger to the purchases ledger control account.

The total of the balances in the purchase ledger is £10,370. The total has been compared with the £11,480 balance on the purchases ledger control account. After investigation the following errors were found:

1. A supplier account with a credit balance of £590 was omitted from the total.

2. A contra entry for £130 has been made in the subsidiary ledger but not in the general ledger.

3. A cash payment to supplier Z was entered into this account as £460 instead of the correct amount of £640.

4. A purchase invoice of £285 was posted to the supplier account as a credit note.

(b) **Use the following table to show the THREE adjustments you need to make to the listing of purchases ledger balances.**

Adjustment	Amount £	Add	Deduct
▼			
▼			
▼			

Drop-down list:

Adjustment for (1)
Adjustment for (2)
Adjustment for (3)
Adjustment for (4)

BPP
LEARNING MEDIA

Task 5

This task is about accounting adjustments and journals.

You are working on the accounting records of a business with a year end of 31 March. A trial balance has been drawn up and a suspense account opened.

You now need to make some corrections and adjustments for the year ended 31 March 20X7.

(a) **Record the necessary adjustments into the extract from the extended trial balance below. You will not need to enter adjustments on every line. Do NOT enter zeros into unused cells.**

(i) An accrual needs to be made for telecommunications costs of £310. Telecommunications costs are classified as office expenses. Ignore VAT.

(ii) A rental receipt of £880 was correctly entered into the rent receivable account, but no other entries have been made. Ignore VAT.

(iii) No entries have been made for closing inventory as at 31 March 20X7. It has been valued at sales price of £19,420. The sales price of goods is always set at 25% higher than the cost of those goods. Ignore VAT.

(iv) The figures from the columns of the sales day-book for 22 March 20X7 have been totalled correctly as follows:

Sales column	£4,700
VAT column	£940
Total column	£5,640

When posting the figures, the entry for VAT was omitted. The other entries were made correctly.

Extract from extended trial balance

Ledger account	Ledger balances		Adjustments	
	Dr £	Cr £	Dr £	Cr £
Accruals				
Bank	2,280			
Closing inventory – statement of financial position				
Closing inventory – profit or loss account				
Disposals of non-current assets		270		
Interest received		114		
Office expenses	16,490			
Office furniture at cost	21,000			
Purchases	208,300			
Purchases ledger control account		20,740		
Rent receivable		3,520		
Sales		260,040		
Sales ledger control account	28,300			
Suspense		60		
VAT		2,350		

The ledgers are now ready to be closed off for the year ended 31 March 20X7.

(b) **Show the correct journal entries to close off the interest received account and select an appropriate narrative.**

Journal

	Dr £	Cr £
▼		
▼		

BPP LEARNING MEDIA

Drop-down list:

Accruals
Bank
Closing inventory – statement of financial position
Closing inventory – statement of profit or loss
Disposals of non-current assets
Interest received
Office expenses
Office furniture at cost
Profit or loss account
Purchases
Purchases ledger control account
Rent receivable
Sales
Sales ledger control account
Statement of financial position
Suspense
VAT

Narrative:

Drop-down list:

Transfer of interest received for year ended 31 March 20X7 to the suspense account

Transfer of interest received for year ended 31 March 20X7 to the bank account

Transfer of interest received for year ended 31 March 20X7 to the statement of financial position

Transfer of interest received for year ended 31 March 20X7 to the statement of profit or loss

•••

Task 6

This task is about preparing an extended trial balance and showing your knowledge of good accounting practice.

You have the following extended trial balance. The adjustments have already been correctly entered.

Extend the figures into the statement of profit or loss (SPL) and statement of financial position (SFP) columns.

Do NOT enter zeros into unused column cells.

Complete the extended trial balance by entering figures and a label in the correct places.

(a) Extended trial balance

Ledger account	Ledger balances		Adjustments		Statement of profit or loss		Statement of financial position	
	Dr £	Cr £	Dr £	Cr £	Dr £	Cr £	Dr £	Cr £
Administration expenses	33,590							
Bank	1,530							
Capital		22,000						
Closing inventory			18,530	18,530				
Depreciation charges	6,075							
Drawings	13,730		1,270					
Opening inventory	16,720							
Payroll costs	29,630			910				
Purchases	171,520			1,270				
Purchases ledger control account		16,100	380					
Rent	14,800							
Sales		287,716	376					
Sales ledger control account	23,840			380				
Sales returns	3,386			376				
Suspense		5,165	6,075	910				
VAT		4,090						
Vehicles at cost	32,400							
Vehicles accumulated depreciation		12,150		6,075				
▼								
TOTAL	347,221	347,221	27,541	27,541	0	0	0	

Drop-down list:

Suspense
Profit/loss for the year
Balance c/d
Gross profit/loss for the year
Balance b/d

A different business is experiencing problems collecting sums owed by customers. It decides to set up an allowance against a specific debt plus a general allowance for doubtful debts.

(b) **Complete the following sentence:**

To account for the uncertainty with the specific debt the [▼] account in the [▼] should be used.

Drop-down list:

allowance for doubtful debts
irrecoverable debts

general ledger
sales ledger

(c) **Which of these statements is true? Choose ONE:**

The weighted average cost method of inventory valuation is the only method acceptable under accounting standards. ☐

Selling costs may be included in the valuation of inventory. ☐

Inventory valuations may include raw materials purchased for making into products for sale. ☐

Inventory is valued at the higher of cost and net realisable value. ☐

A different business has a large debit balance in its bash book. Its VAT control account always shows tax on sales greater than tax on purchases.

The quarterly VAT account is settled by means of an automated bank transaction.

(d) **Tick the boxes to show what effect this transaction will have on the elements of the accounting equation shown below.**

You must choose ONE answer for EACH row.

	Increase	Decrease	No change
Assets	☐	☐	☐
Liabilities	☐	☐	☐
Capital	☐	☐	☐

AAT AQ2013 SAMPLE ASSESSMENT 2 ACCOUNTS PREPARATION

ANSWERS

Task 1

Extract from non-current assets register

Description/ Serial Number	Acquisition Date	Cost £	Depreciation charges £	Carrying amount £	Funding method	Disposal Proceeds £	Disposal date
Office equipment							
Copier 4	01/04/X5	3,200.00			Finance lease		
Year end 31/03/X6			400.00	2,800.00			
Year end 31/03/X7			400.00	2,400.00			
Reception desk – FaradyR	01/01/X5	1,200.00			Cash		
Year end 31/03/X5			37.50	1,162.50			
Year end 31/03/X6			150.00	1,012.50			
Year end 31/03/X7			75.00 	Nil 		600.00	30/09/X6
Machinery							
CNC machine CNC3491	01/04/X4	16,400.00			Part-exchange		
Year end 31/03/X5			4,100.00	12,300.00			
Year end 31/03/X6			3,075.00	9,225.00			
Year end 31/03/X7			2,306.25	6,918.75			
Power lathe PM892	01/04/X6	10,189.80			Hire purchase		
Year end 31/03/X7			2,547.45	7,642.35			

Task 2

(a) **Calculate the depreciation charge for the year on the new machine.**

£ [1,975]

(b) and (c)

Machinery at cost

	£			£
Balance b/d	42,800	Balance c/d	▼	52,100
Bank ▼	9,300		▼	
▼			▼	
	52,100			52,100

Depreciation charges

	£			£
Balance b/d	9,630	Profit or loss account	▼	11,605
Machinery accumulated depreciation ▼	1,975		▼	
▼			▼	
	11,605			11,605

Machinery accumulated depreciation

	£			£
Balance c/d ▼	21,235	Balance b/d		19,260
▼		Depreciation charges ▼	1,975	
▼			▼	
	21,235			21,235

BPP
LEARNING MEDIA

An item of computer equipment originally purchased for £2,700 and with a carrying amount of £675 has been sold. The loss on disposal was £150. A cheque for the proceeds was banked.

(d) **How much did the business receive for the computer equipment? Ignore VAT.**

£ | 525 |

(e) **Which ONE of the following is the main purpose of a non-current asset register?**

To provide internal control. ✓

To provide the selling price of a particular item at the time of its disposal. ☐

To provide a measure of financial performance. ☐

Task 3

(a) **Show how the general ledger account for general expenses looked at the beginning of the financial year. Insert ONE date, ONE description and ONE amount into the correct position in the ledger account.**

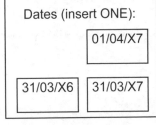

Dates (insert ONE):

01/04/X7

31/03/X6 | 31/03/X7

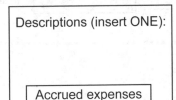

Descriptions (insert ONE):

Accrued expenses b/d

Amounts (insert ONE):

1,350

General expenses

Date	Description	Dr £	Date	Description	Cr £
01/04/X6	Prepaid expenses b/d	2,100			

(b) **Complete the following statement:**

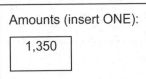

On 31/03/X7, the general expenses account shows a | debit ▾ | entry for

| Accrued expenses ▾ | carried down of £ | 1,350 | .

(c) **Calculate the general expenses for the year ended 31/03/X7.**

£ [16,250]

(d) **Update the vehicle running expenses account for this, showing clearly the balance to be carried down.**

Vehicle running expenses

		£			£
Bank	▼	23,700	Accrued expenses b/d		1,970
	▼		Balance c/d	▼	21,730
	▼			▼	
		23,700			23,700

You now find out that the cash book figure for vehicle running expenses includes £375 relating to the period 01/02/X7 to 30/04/X7.

(e) **Taking into account this information, complete the following statement:**

The amount to be transferred to the statement of profit or loss for vehicle running expenses will be £ [125] [less ▼] than the figure carried down in answer (d) above.

BPP
LEARNING MEDIA

Task 4

(a) Using all the information given above and the figures given in the table below, enter amounts in the appropriate trial balance columns for the accounts shown.

Do NOT enter zeros in unused column cells. Do NOT enter any figures as negatives.

Extract from the trial balance as at 31 March 20X7	Ledger balance	Trial balance	
Account	**£**	**£ Dr**	**£ Cr**
Allowance for doubtful debts adjustment			80
Capital	30,000		30,000
Disposal of non-current assets		780	
Insurance costs		1,300	
Loan		1,000	
Loan interest received	50		50
Miscellaneous income			2,537
Payroll expenses	9,600	9,600	
Prepaid expenses		325	

(b) Use the following table to show the THREE adjustments you need to make to the listing of purchases ledger balances.

Adjustment		Amount £	Add	Deduct
Adjustment for (1)	▼	590	✓	
Adjustment for (3)	▼	180		✓
Adjustment for (4)	▼	570	✓	

Task 5

(a) Extract from extended trial balance

Ledger account	Ledger balances		Adjustments	
	Dr £	Cr £	Dr £	Cr £
Accruals				310
Bank	2,280		880	
Closing inventory – statement of financial position			15,536	
Closing inventory – profit or loss account				15,536
Disposals of non-current assets		270		
Interest received		114		
Office expenses	16,490		310	
Office furniture at cost	21,000			
Purchases	208,300			
Purchases ledger control account		20,740		
Rent receivable		3,520		
Sales		260,040		
Sales ledger control account	28,300			
Suspense		60	940	880
VAT		2,350		940

The ledgers are now ready to be closed off for the year ended 31 March 20X7.

(b) Show the correct journal entries to close off the interest received account and select an appropriate narrative.

Journal

		Dr £	Cr £
Interest received	▼	114	
Profit or loss account	▼		114

Narrative:

Transfer of interest received for year ended 31 March 20X7 to the statement of profit or loss	▼

BPP
LEARNING MEDIA

Task 6

(a) Extended trial balance

Ledger account	Ledger balances		Adjustments		Statement of profit or loss		Statement of financial position	
	Dr £	Cr £	Dr £	Cr £	Dr £	Cr £	Dr £	Cr £
Administration expenses	33,590				33,590			
Bank	1,530						1,530	
Capital		22,000						22,000
Closing inventory			18,530	18,530		18,530	18,530	
Depreciation charges	6,075				6,075			
Drawings	13,730		1,270				15,000	
Opening inventory	16,720				16,720			
Payroll costs	29,630		910		30,540			
Purchases	171,520			1,270	170,250			
Purchases ledger control account		16,100	380					15,720
Rent	14,800				14,800			
Sales		287,716	376			287,340		
Sales ledger control account	23,840			380			23,460	
Sales returns	3,386			376	3,010			
Suspense		5,165	6,075	910				
VAT		4,090						4,090
Vehicles at cost	32,400						32,400	
Vehicles accumulated depreciation		12,150		6,075				18,225
Profit/loss for the year ▼					30,885			30,885
TOTAL	347,221	347,221	27,541	27,541	305,870	305,870	90,920	90,920

(b) Complete the following sentence:

To account for the uncertainty with the specific debt the

| allowance for doubtful debts ▼ | account in the | general ledger ▼ | should be used.

(c) **Which of these statements is true? Choose ONE:**

The weighted average cost method of inventory valuation is the only method acceptable under accounting standards. ☐

Selling costs may be included in the valuation of inventory. ☐

Inventory valuations may include raw materials purchased for making into products for sale. ☑

Inventory is valued at the higher of cost and net realisable value. ☐

(d) **Tick the boxes to show what effect this transaction will have on the elements of the accounting equation shown below.**

You must choose ONE answer for EACH row.

	Increase	Decrease	No change
Assets	☐	☑	☐
Liabilities	☐	☑	☐
Capital	☐	☐	☑

BPP
LEARNING MEDIA

BPP PRACTICE ASSESSMENT 1
ACCOUNTS PREPARATION

Time allowed: 2 hours

Task 1

This task is about recording information for non-current assets for a business known as Rootle Ltd. Rootle Ltd is registered for VAT and its year-end is 30 September.

The following is a purchase invoice received by Rootle Ltd:

Fittings Supplies plc Unit 76 East Trading Estate Mendlesham ME2 9FG	Invoice 9032	Date:	20 June X5
To:	Rootle Ltd 14 Larkmead Road Mendlesham ME6 2PO		
Description	Item number	Quantity	£
Warehouse racking system	WR617	1	2000.00
Delivery and set-up charges		1	200.00
Specialist oil for racking @ £15.00 per litre		3 litres	45.00
Net			2245.00
VAT @ 20%			449.00
Total			2694.00
Settlement terms: strictly 30 days net.			

The following information relates to the sale of an item of machinery:

Identification number	MC5267
Date of sale	22 June X5
Selling price excluding VAT	£3,250.00

- Rootle Ltd's policy is to recognise items of capital expenditure over £200 as non-current assets.

- Furniture and fittings are depreciated at 25% using the straight line method. There are no residual values.

- Machinery is depreciated at 40% using the diminishing balance method.

- A full year's depreciation is charged in the year of acquisition and none in the year of sale.

Record the following information in the non-current assets register below:

(a) Any acquisitions of non-current assets during the year ended 30 September X5
(b) Any disposals of non-current assets during the year ended 30 September X5
(c) Depreciation for the year ended 30 September X5

Non-current assets register

Description	Acquisition date	Cost £	Depreciation charges £	Carrying amount £	Funding method	Disposal proceeds £	Disposal date
Furniture and fittings							
Warehouse racking systems							
WR290							
Year end 30/09/X3	1/12/X2	6,000.00	1,500.00	4,500.00	Credit		
Year end 30/09/X4			1,500.00	3,000.00			
Year end 30/09/X5							
WR617							
Year end 30/09/X5							
Machinery							
MC5267					Cash		
Year end 30/09/X3	1/10/X2	7,500.00	3,000.00	4,500.00			
Year end 30/09/X4			1,800.00	2,700.00			
Year end 30/09/X5							
MC5298					Credit		
Year end 30/09/X4	31/01/X4	8,800.00	3,520.00	5,280.00			
Year end 30/09/X5							

BPP
LEARNING MEDIA

Task 2

This task is about recording non-current asset information in the general ledger and other non-current asset matters.

- You are working on the accounts of a sole trader who is registered for VAT. The business's year end is 31 December 20XX.

- On 1 September 20XX the business bought a new machine for the business on which VAT can be reclaimed.

- The machine cost £12,200 excluding VAT. An invoice has been received from the seller which has been recorded in the purchases day book.

- The machine's residual value is expected to be £2,300 excluding VAT.

- The business's depreciation policy for machines is 10% per annum on a straight line basis. A full year's depreciation is charged in the year of acquisition and none in the year of disposal.

- Depreciation has already been entered into the accounts for the business's existing machines.

Make entries to account for:

(a) **The purchase of the new machine**
(b) **The depreciation on the new machine**

On each account, show clearly the balance carried down or transferred to the statement of profit or loss.

Machines at cost

	£		£
Balance b/d	20,000		

Machines accumulated depreciation

	£		£
		Balance b/d	8,600

Depreciation charge

	£		£
Balance b/d	5,700		

(c) When non-current assets are depreciated using the diminishing balance method, an equal amount is charged for each year of the asset's life.

✓	
	True
	False

Task 3

This task is about accounting for accruals and prepayments and preparing a trial balance.

You are working on the final accounts of a business for the year ended 30 June 20X4. In this task, you can ignore VAT.

You have the following information:

Balances as at:	1 July 20X3 £
Accrual of rental income	250
Prepayment of selling expenses	87

The bank summary for the year shows receipts of rental income of £5,000. Included in this figure is £270 for the quarter ended 31 July 20X4.

(a) **Prepare the rental income account for the year ended 30 June 20X4 and close it off by showing the transfer to the statement of profit or loss.**

Rental income

Details	£	Details	£

The bank summary for the year shows payments for selling expenses of £2,850. In June 20X4, £63 was paid for items delivered and used in July 20X4.

(b) **Prepare the selling expenses account for the year ended 30 June 20X4 and close it off by showing the transfer to the statement of profit or loss. Include dates.**

BPP
LEARNING MEDIA

Selling expenses

Date	Details	£	Date	Details	£

Task 4

This task is about preparing a trial balance and reconciliations.

You are working on the accounts of a business with a year end of 30 June. You have five extracts from the ledger accounts as at 30 June 20X4. You need to start preparing the trial balance as at 30 June 20X4.

(a) **Using all the information given below and the figures given in the table, enter amounts in the appropriate trial balance columns for the accounts shown.**

Do NOT enter zeros in unused column cells.

Do NOT enter any figures as negatives.

Bank

		£	30/06/X4	Balance b/f	£ 10,460

Disposal of non-current asset

		£	30/06/X4	Balance b/f	£ 700

Interest received

		£	30/06/X4	Balance b/f	£ 3,250

This balance has been adjusted for interest received in advance of £240 as at 30/06/X4.

Telecommunication costs

30/06/X4	Balance b/f	£ 5,960			£

This balance has been adjusted for prepaid expenses of £329 as at 30/06/X4.

VAT

		£	30/06/X4	Balance b/f	£ 7,230

Extract from trial balance as at 30 June 20X4

Account	£	Debit £	Credit £
Accrued expenses			
Accrued income			
Capital	10,000		
Irrecoverable debts expense	780		
Discounts received	1,209		
Interest expense	201		
Disposal of non-current asset			
Bank			
Interest received			
Telecommunications costs			
VAT			
Prepaid expenses			
Prepaid income			

(b) **Use the following information to complete the table below to show the THREE adjustments you need to make to the sales ledger control account.**

The balance on the sales ledger control account has been compared with the total of the list of sales ledger accounts and the following differences have been identified:

1. The sales ledger column in the cash receipts book was undercast by £100.

2. A contra for £76 was only recorded in the sales ledger.

3. An invoice for £563 in the sales day book was not posted to the sales ledger.

4. A total in the sales returns day book of £489 was recorded in the general ledger as £498.

BPP LEARNING MEDIA

The balance showing on the sales ledger control account is £5,097 and the total of the list of sales ledger balances is £4,367.

Adjustment	Amount £	Debit ✓	Credit ✓

Task 5

This task is about recording journal entries.

You are working on the final accounts of a business with a year end of 31 December. A trial balance has been drawn up and a suspense account opened with a credit balance of £2,243. You now need to make some corrections and adjustments for the year ended 31 December 20X4.

Record the journal entries needed in the general ledger to deal with the items below.

You should:

- **Remove any incorrect entries, where appropriate**
- **Post the correct entries**

You do not need to give narratives.

Do NOT enter zeros into unused column cells.

Ignore VAT.

(a) Entries needed to increase the allowance for receivables from £1,524 to £2,887.

Journal

Account name	Debit £	Credit £

(b) A fully depreciated vehicle has been sold for £1,986. Only the cash book has been updated for this transaction.

Journal

Account name	Debit £	Credit £

(c) Discounts received of £257 have only been entered into the purchases ledger control account from the cash payments book.

Journal

Account name	Debit £	Credit £

(d) When posting from the purchases returns day book, the entries for credit notes totalling £459 have been made to the wrong sides of both the relevant accounts.

Journal

Account name	Debit £	Credit £

BPP
LEARNING MEDIA

Task 6

This task is about completing an extended trial balance and showing your accounting knowledge.

You have the following extended trial balance. The adjustments have already been correctly entered.

(a) **Extend the figures into the statement of profit or loss and statement of financial position columns.**

Do NOT enter zeros into unused column cells.

Make the columns balance by entering figures and a label in the correct places.

Extended trial balance

Ledger account	Ledger balances		Adjustments		Statement of profit or loss		Statement of financial position	
	£	£	£	£	£	£	£	£
Allowance for doubtful debts		1,347		203				
Allowance for doubtful debts adjustment			203					
Bank		5,290						
Capital		9,460						
Closing inventory			7,234	7,234				
Depreciation charge			7,800					
Administration expenses	6,739			569				
Opening inventory	9,933							
Wages and salaries	29,378			6,000				
Purchases	34,289							
Purchases ledger control account		5,096						
Sales		112,015		3,000				
Sales ledger control account	8,023							
Marketing	7,365							
Suspense		8,819	9,569	750				
VAT		6,300						
Machinery at cost	115,000		750					
Machinery accumulated depreciation		62,400		7,800				
	210,727	210,727	25,556	25,556				

(b) **The rule for valuing inventory is to use**

✓	
	The lower of FIFO and LIFO
	The lower of cost and net realisable value
	The lower of FIFO and net realisable value
	The lower of cost and LIFO

BPP
LEARNING MEDIA

BPP PRACTICE ASSESSMENT 1
ACCOUNTS PREPARATION

ANSWERS

Task 1

(a) – (c)

Non-current assets register

Description	Acquisition date	Cost £	Depreciation charges £	Carrying amount £	Funding method	Disposal proceeds £	Disposal date
Furniture and fittings							
Warehouse racking systems							
WR290							
Year end 30/09/X3	1/12/X2	6,000.00	1,500.00	4,500.00	Credit		
Year end 30/09/X4			1,500.00	3,000.00			
Year end 30/09/X5			**1,500.00**	**1,500.00**			
WR617							
	20/06/X5	**2,200.00**					
Year end 30/09/X5			**550.00**	**1,650.00**	**Credit**		
Machinery							
MC5267					Cash		
Year end 30/09/X3	1/10/X2	7,500.00	3,000.00	4,500.00			
Year end 30/09/X4			1,800.00	2,700.00			
Year end 30/09/X5			0.00	0.00		**3,250.00**	**22/06/X5**
MC5298					Credit		
Year end 30/09/X4	31/01/X4	8,800.00	3,520.00	5,280.00			
Year end 30/09/X5			**2,112.00**	**3,168.00**			

Task 2

(a) and (b)

Machines at cost

	£		£
Balance b/d	20,000	**Balance c/d**	**32,200**
Purchases ledger control	**12,200**		
	32,200		**32,200**

Machines accumulated depreciation

	£		£
Balance c/d	**9,590**	Balance b/d	8,600
		Depreciation charge	**990**
	9,590		**9,590**

Depreciation charge

	£		£
Balance b/d	5,700	**Statement of profit or loss**	**6,690**
Machines accumulated depreciation	**990**		
	6,690		**6,690**

(c)

✓	
	True
✓	False

....

Task 3

(a) **Rental income**

Details	£	Details	£
Balance b/d	250	**Bank**	**5,000**
Balance c/d	90		
Statement of profit or loss	4,660		
	5,000		**5,000**

BPP
LEARNING MEDIA

(b) Selling expenses

Date	Details	£	Date	Details	£
1/7	Balance b/d	87	30/6	Balance c/d	63
30/6	Bank	2,850	30/6	Statement of profit or loss	2,874
		2,937			2,937

Task 4

(a) Extract from trial balance as at 30 June 20X4

Account	£	Debit £	Credit £
Accrued expenses			
Accrued income			
Capital	10,000		10,000
Irrecoverable debts expense	780	780	
Discounts received	1,209		
Interest expense	201	201	
Disposal of non-current asset			700
Bank			10,460
Interest received			3,250
Telecommunications costs		5,960	
VAT			7,230
Prepaid expenses		329	
Prepaid income			240

(b)

Adjustment	Amount £	Debit ✓	Credit ✓
Adjustment for 1	100		✓
Adjustment for 2	76		✓
Adjustment for 4	9	✓	

Task 5

(a) Journal

Account name	Debit £	Credit £
Allowance for doubtful debts adjustment	1,363	
Allowance for doubtful debts		1,363

(b) Journal

Account name	Debit £	Credit £
Suspense account	1,986	
Disposals		1,986

(c) Journal

Account name	Debit £	Credit £
Suspense account	257	
Discounts received		257

(d) Journal

Account name	Debit £	Credit £
Purchases ledger control	459	
Purchases returns		459
Purchases ledger control	459	
Purchases returns		459

BPP LEARNING MEDIA

Task 6

(a) Extended trial balance

Ledger account	Ledger balances		Adjustments		Statement of profit or loss		Statement of financial position	
	£	£	£	£	£	£	£	£
Allowance for doubtful debts		1,347		203				1,550
Allowance for doubtful debts adjustment			203		203			
Bank		5,290						5,290
Capital		9,460						9,460
Closing inventory			7,234	7,234		7,234	7,234	
Depreciation charge			7,800		7,800			
Administration expenses	6,739			569	6,170			
Opening inventory	9,933				9,933			
Wages and salaries	29,378			6,000	23,378			
Purchases	34,289				34,289			
Purchases ledger control account		5,096						5,096
Sales		112,015		3,000		115,015		
Sales ledger control account	8,023						8,023	
Marketing	7,365				7,365			
Suspense		8,819	9,569	750				
VAT		6,300						6,300
Machinery at cost	115,000		750				115,750	
Machinery accumulated depreciation		62,400		7,800				70,200
Profit for the year					33,111			33,111
	210,727	210,727	25,556	25,556	122,249	122,249	131,007	131,007

191

(b)

✓	
	The lower of FIFO and LIFO
✓	The lower of cost and net realisable value
	The lower of FIFO and net realisable value
	The lower of cost and LIFO

BPP
LEARNING MEDIA

BPP PRACTICE ASSESSMENT 2
ACCOUNTS PREPARATION

Time allowed: 2 hours

PRACTICE ASSESSMENT 2

Task 1

This task is about recording information for non-current assets for a business known as Hagbourne & Co. The business is registered for VAT and its year end is 31 March.

The following is a purchase invoice received by Hagbourne & Co:

Office Supplies Ltd 28 High Street Cridley CR4 6AS	Invoice 198233	Date:	1 December 20X5
To:	Hagbourne & Co 67 Foggarty Street Cridley CR9 0TT		
Description	Item number	Quantity	£
Modular office workstation system	OFF783	1	3,500.00
Delivery and assembly charges		1	100.00
Printer paper		75 reams	200.00
Net			3,800.00
VAT @ 20%			760.00
Total			4,560.00
Settlement terms: strictly 30 days net.			

The following information relates to the sale of a motor vehicle:

Identification number	CR05 KJH
Date of sale	1 April 20X5
Selling price excluding VAT	£7,400.00

- Hagbourne & Co's policy is to recognise items of capital expenditure over £100 as non-current assets.

- Office equipment is depreciated at 20% per annum using the straight line method. A residual value of 25% of cost is assumed.

- Motor vehicles are depreciated at 40% per annum using the diminishing balance method.

- A full year's depreciation is charged in the year of acquisition, none in the year of disposal.

Record the following information in the non-current assets register below:

(a) Any acquisitions of non-current assets during the year ended 31 March 20X6
(b) Any disposals of non-current assets during the year ended 31 March 20X6
(c) Depreciation for the year ended 31 March 20X6

Non-current assets register

Description	Acquisition date	Cost £	Depreciation charges £	Carrying amount £	Funding method	Disposal proceeds £	Disposal date
Motor vehicles							
CR04 YTR							
Year end 31/3/X4	1/4/X3	18,000.00	7,200.00	10,800.00	Credit		
Year end 31/3/X5			4,320.00	6,480.00			
Year end 31/3/X6							
CR05 KJH					Credit		
Year end 31/3/X5	1/4/X4	10,540.00	4,216.00	6,324.00			
Year end 31/3/X6							
Office equipment							
OFF253							
Year end 31/3/X4	1/1/X4	10,000.00	1,500.00	8,500.00	Cash		
Year end 31/3/X5			1,500.00	7,000.00			
Year end 31/3/X6							
OFF783							
Year end 31/3/X6							

Task 2

This task is about recording non-current asset information in the general ledger and other non-current asset matters.

- You are working on the accounts of a business which is not registered for VAT. The business's year end is 31 December 20X6.

- On 1 January 20X6 the business sold some machinery for £750. This amount has already been entered in the cash book.

- The machinery cost £2,000 on 1 January 20X3.

- The business's depreciation policy for machinery is 20% using the diminishing balance method.

(a) **Make entries to account for the disposal of the machine.**

   On each account, show clearly the balance carried down or transferred to the statement of profit or loss.

Machines at cost

Balance b/d	15,000		

Machines accumulated depreciation

		Balance b/d	9,200

Disposal account

(b) **A non-current asset is disposed of and a part exchange allowance is given in respect of a new non-current asset. The amount of the allowance is:**

✓	
	Debited to the disposal account and credited to the non-current asset cost account
	Debited to the non-current asset cost account and credited to the disposal account

Task 3

This task is about accounting for accruals and prepayments and preparing a trial balance.

You are working on the final accounts of a business for the year ended 30 September 20X6. In this task, you can ignore VAT.

You have the following information:

Balances as at:	1 October 20X5 £
Prepayment of commission income	175
Accrual of stationery	134

The bank summary for the year shows receipts of commission income of £496. Commission of £63 is still due for September 20X6 at the year end.

(a) **Prepare the commission income account for the year ended 30 September 20X6 and close it off by showing the transfer to the statement of profit or loss.**

Commission income

Details	£	Details	£

The bank summary for the year shows payments for stationery of £798. In September 20X6, £48 was paid for items delivered and used in October 20X6.

(b) **Prepare the stationery account for the year ended 30 September 20X6 and close it off by showing the transfer to the statement of profit or loss. Include dates.**

BPP LEARNING MEDIA

Stationery

Date	Details	£	Date	Details	£

....

Task 4

This task is about preparing a trial balance and reconciliations.

You are working on the accounts of a business with a year end of 30 September. You have five extracts from the ledger accounts as at 30 September 20X6. You need to start preparing the trial balance as at 30 September 20X6.

(a) **Using all the information given below and the figures given in the table, enter amounts in the appropriate trial balance columns for the accounts shown.**

Do NOT enter zeros in unused column cells.

Do NOT enter any figures as negatives.

Allowance for doubtful debts adjustment

		£		£
30/09/X6	Balance b/f	230		

Disposal of non-current asset

		£			£
			30/09/X6	Balance b/f	500

Office costs

		£		£
30/09/X6	Balance b/f	3,660		

Included in this balance is an amount for accrued expenses of £420 as at 30/09/X6.

Recycling rebates

		£			£
			30/09/X6	Balance b/f	4,927

Included in this balance is an amount for accrued income of £750 as at 30/09/X6.

VAT

		£			£
			30/09/X6	Balance b/f	2,993

Extract from trial balance as at 30 September 20X6

Account	£	Debit £	Credit £
Accrued expenses			
Accrued income			
Drawings	2,500		
Purchases returns	1,982		
Allowance for doubtful debts adjustment			
Disposal of non-current asset			
Office costs			
Recycling rebates			
VAT			
Prepaid expenses			
Prepaid income			

(b) The balance on the purchases ledger control account has been compared with the total of the list of purchases ledger accounts and the following differences have been identified:

1. Total discounts received of £1,489 were only recorded in the discounts received account.

2. A purchases ledger column of £1,267 in the cash payments book was not posted to the purchases ledger control account.

3. A contra for £123 was only recorded in the purchases ledger control account.

4. The total column in the purchases returns day book was overcast by £180.

The balance showing on the purchases ledger control account is £7,092 and the total of the list of purchases ledger balances is £4,639.

BPP LEARNING MEDIA

Use the following table to show the THREE adjustments you need to make to the purchases ledger control account.

Adjustment	Amount £	Debit ✓	Credit ✓

Task 5

This task is about recording adjustments in the extended trial balance and closing off accounts.

You are working on the final accounts of a business with a year end of 31 December 20X6. A trial balance has been drawn up and a suspense account opened with a debit balance of £3,526. You now need to make some corrections and adjustments for the year ended 31 December 20X6.

(a) **Record the adjustments needed on the extract from the extended trial balance to deal with the items below.**

You will not need to enter adjustments on every line. Do NOT enter zeros into unused cells.

(i) Entries need to be made for an irrecoverable debt of £672.

(ii) Drawings of £850 have been made. The correct entry was made in the cash book but no other entries were made.

(iii) Closing inventory for the year end 31 December 20X6 has not yet been recorded. Its value at cost is £9,350. Included in this figure are some items costing £345 that will be sold for £200.

(iv) Credit notes of £1,338 have been posted to the correct side of the sales ledger control account, but have been made to the same side of the sales returns account.

Extract from extended trial balance

	Ledger balances		Adjustments	
	Debit £	Credit £	Debit £	Credit £
Allowance for doubtful debts adjustment		134		
Bank	7,826			
Closing inventory – SFP				
Closing inventory – SPL				
Drawings				
Irrecoverable debts				
Plant and machinery – accumulated depreciation		19,800		
Purchases returns		2,781		
Purchases ledger control account		92,831		
Sales		169,200		
Sales returns	5,421			
Sales ledger control account	12,569			
Suspense	3,526			

(b) **The ledgers are ready to be closed off for the year ended 31 December 20X6. Show the correct entries to close off the allowance for doubtful debts adjustment account and insert an appropriate narrative.**

Account	Debit ✓	Credit ✓

BPP LEARNING MEDIA

Task 6

This task is about completing an extended trial balance and showing your accounting knowledge.

You have the following extended trial balance. The adjustments have already been correctly entered.

(a) **Extend the figures into the statement of profit or loss and statement of financial position columns.**

Do NOT enter zeros into unused column cells.

Make the columns balance by entering figures and a label in the correct places.

Extended trial balance

Ledger account	Ledger balances		Adjustments		Statement of profit or loss		Statement of financial position	
	£	£	£	£	£	£	£	£
Bank	5,246							
Capital		19,600						
Closing inventory			6,712	6,712				
Depreciation charge	4,298		4,000					
Discounts received		2,291		1,325				
Drawings	11,712		9,826					
Irrecoverable debts	627							
Motor expenses	2,065							
Motor vehicles accumulated depreciation		12,500		4,000				
Motor vehicles at cost	20,000							
Office expenses	7,219							
Opening inventory	4,820							
Purchases	91,289							
Purchases ledger control account		7,109	786					
Salaries	32,781		3,484					
Sales		156,782						
Sales ledger control account	11,092							
Suspense	12,771		1,325	14,096				
VAT		5,638						
	203,920	203,920	26,133	26,133				

(b) **To reduce the allowance for doubtful debts we must:**

✓	
	Credit the allowance for doubtful debts account
	Debit the irrecoverable debts account
	Credit the allowance for doubtful debts adjustment account
	Credit the sales ledger control account
	None of the above

BPP
LEARNING MEDIA

BPP PRACTICE ASSESSMENT 2
ACCOUNTS PREPARATION

ANSWERS

Task 1

(a) – (b)

Non-current assets register

Description	Acquisition date	Cost £	Depreciation charges £	Carrying amount £	Funding method	Disposal proceeds £	Disposal date
Motor vehicles							
CR04 YTR							
Year end 31/3/X4	1/4/X3	18,000.00	7,200.00	10,800.00	Credit		
Year end 31/3/X5			4,320.00	6,480.00			
Year end 31/3/X6			**2,592.00**	**3,888.00**			
CR05 KJH							
Year end 31/3/X5	1/4/X4	10,540.00	4,216.00	6,324.00	Credit		
Year end 31/3/X6			0.00	0.00		7,400.00	1/4/X5
Office equipment							
OFF253							
Year end 31/3/X4	1/1/X4	10,000.00	1,500.00	8,500.00	Cash		
Year end 31/3/X5			1,500.00	7,000.00			
Year end 31/3/X6			**1,500.00**	**5,500.00**			
OFF783	**1/12/X5**	**3,600.00**			**Credit**		
Year end 31/3/X6			**540.00**	**3,060.00**			

Task 2

(a)

Machines at cost

Balance b/d	15,000	Disposal account	**2,000**
	_____	Balance c/d	**13,000**
	15,000		15,000

Machines accumulated depreciation

Disposal account	**976**	Balance b/d	9,200
Balance c/d	**8,224**		_____
	9,200		9,200

Disposal account

Machines at cost	**2,000**	**Machines accumulated depreciation**	**976**
		Bank	**750**
	_____	**Statement of profit or loss**	**274**
	2,000		2,000

(b)

✓	
	Debited to the disposal account and credited to the non-current asset cost account
✓	Debited to the non-current asset cost account and credited to the disposal account

Task 3

(a) Commission income

Details	£	Details	£
Statement of profit or loss	734	Balance b/d	175
		Bank	496
	——	Balance c/d	63
	734		734

(b) Stationery

Date	Details	£	Date	Details	£
30/9	Bank	798	1/10	Balance b/d	134
			30/9	Balance c/d	48
		——	30/9	Statement of profit or loss	616
		798			798

Task 4

(a) **Extract from trial balance as at 30 September 20X6**

Account	£	Debit £	Credit £
Accrued expenses			420
Accrued income		750	
Drawings	2,500	2,500	
Purchases returns	1,982		1,982
Allowance for doubtful debts adjustment		230	
Disposal of non-current asset			500
Office costs		3,660	
Recycling rebates			4,927
VAT			2,993
Prepaid expenses			
Prepaid income			

(b)

Adjustment	Amount £	Debit ✓	Credit ✓
Adjustment for 1	1,489	✓	
Adjustment for 2	1,267	✓	
Adjustment for 4	180		✓

BPP
LEARNING MEDIA

Task 5

(a) Extract from extended trial balance

	Ledger balances		Adjustments	
	Debit	Credit	Debit	Credit
	£	£	£	£
Allowance for doubtful debts adjustment		134		
Bank	7,826			
Closing inventory – SFP			9,205	
Closing inventory – SPL				9,205
Drawings			850	
Irrecoverable debts			672	
Plant and machinery – accumulated depreciation		19,800		
Purchases returns		2,781		
Purchases ledger control account		92,831		
Sales		169,200		
Sales returns	5,421		2,676	
Sales ledger control account	12,569			672
Suspense	3,526			3,526

(b)

Account	Debit ✓	Credit ✓
Allowance for doubtful debts adjustment	134	
Statement of profit or loss		134
Transfer of allowance for doubtful debts adjustment for year ended 31 December 20X6 to statement of profit or loss.		

Task 6

(a) Extended trial balance

Ledger account	Ledger balances		Adjustments		Statement of profit or loss		Statement of financial position	
	£	£	£	£	£	£	£	£
Bank	5,246						5,246	
Capital		19,600						19,600
Closing inventory			6,712	6,712		6,712	6,712	
Depreciation charge	4,298		4,000		8,298			
Discounts received		2,291		1,325		3,616		
Drawings	11,712		9,826				21,538	
Irrecoverable debts	627				627			
Motor expenses	2,065				2,065			
Motor vehicles accumulated depreciation		12,500		4,000				16,500
Motor vehicles at cost	20,000						20,000	
Office expenses	7,219				7,219			
Opening inventory	4,820				4,820			
Purchases	91,289				91,289			
Purchases ledger control account		7,109	786					6,323
Salaries	32,781		3,484		36,265			
Sales		156,782				156,782		
Sales ledger control account	11,092						11,092	
Suspense	12,771		1,325	14,096				
VAT		5,638						5,638
Profit/loss for the year					16,527			16,527
	203,920	203,920	26,133	26,133	167,110	167,110	64,588	64,588

(b)

✓	
	Credit the allowance for doubtful debts account
	Debit the irrecoverable debts account
✓	Credit the allowance for doubtful debts adjustment account
	Credit the sales ledger control account
	None of the above

BPP PRACTICE ASSESSMENT 3
ACCOUNTS PREPARATION

Time allowed: 2 hours

Task 1

This task is about recording information for non-current assets for a business known as Tilling Brothers. The business is registered for VAT and its year end is 31 December.

The following is a purchase invoice received by Tilling Brothers:

Prestatyn Machinery Ltd 82 Main Road Perwith PE5 9LA	Invoice 654723	Date:	1 May 20X3
To:	Tilling Brothers 56 Kerrick Street Perwith PE4 7PA		
Description	Item number	Quantity	£
Press machine	MAC637	1	8,640.00
Delivery and set-up charges		1	300.00
Maintenance pack (1 year)		1	184.00
Net			9,124.00
VAT @ 20%			1,824.80
Total			10,948.80
Settlement terms: strictly 30 days net.			

The following information relates to the sale of a computer:

Identification number	COM265
Date of sale	1 January 20X3
Selling price excluding VAT	£850.00

- Tilling Brothers' policy is to recognise items of capital expenditure over £200 as non-current assets.

- Machinery is depreciated at 25% using the straight line method with a full year's charge in the year of purchase and none in the year of sale.

- Computer equipment is depreciated at 30% per annum using the diminishing balance method.

Record the following information in the non-current assets register below:

(a) Any acquisitions of non-current assets during the year ended 31 December 20X3.

(b) Any disposals of non-current assets during the year ended 31 December 20X3.

(c) Depreciation for the year ended 31 December 20X3.

Non-current assets register

Description	Acquisition date	Cost £	Depreciation charges £	Carrying amount £	Funding method	Disposal proceeds £	Disposal date
Computer equipment							
COM265							
Year end 31/12/X1	1/1/X1	5,600.00	1,680.00	3,920.00	Credit		
Year end 31/12/X2			1,176.00	2,744.00			
Year end 31/12/X3							
COM399					Credit		
Year end 31/12/X2	1/1/X2	7,200.00	2,160.00	5,040.00			
Year end 31/12/X3							
Machinery							
MAC434							
Year end 31/12/X1	1/7/X1	12,940.00	3,235.00	9,705.00	Credit		
Year end 31/12/X2			3,235.00	6,470.00			
Year end 31/12/X3							
Year end 31/12/X3							

BPP
LEARNING MEDIA

Task 2

This task is about recording non-current asset information in the general ledger and other non-current asset matters.

- You are working on the accounts of a business which is not registered for VAT. The business's year end is 31 December 20X3.

- On 1 January 20X3 the business part exchanged an old machine for a new one with a list price of £3,500. A cheque for £1,000 was paid in full and final settlement and this amount has already been entered in the cash book.

- The old machine cost £4,000 on 1 January 20X1.

- The business's depreciation policy for machinery is 20% using the diminishing balance method.

(a) **Make entries to account for the disposal of the old machine and acquisition of the new one.**

On each account, show clearly the balance carried down or transferred to the statement of profit or loss.

Machines at cost

	£		£
Balance b/d	12,500		

Machines accumulated depreciation

	£		£
		Balance b/d	4,500

Disposal account

	£		£

(b) **When a non-current asset is acquired by paying a regular monthly amount over a set period and then having ownership transferred at the end of that period, the funding method is described as:**

✓	
	Cash purchase
	Hire purchase
	Borrowing
	Part exchange

Task 3

This task is about accounting for accruals and prepayments and preparing a trial balance.

You are working on the final accounts of a business for the year ended 31 December 20X3. In this task, you can ignore VAT.

You have the following information:

Balances as at:	1 January 20X3 £
Accrual of rental income	1,000
Accrual of heat and light	345

The bank summary for the year shows receipts of rental income of £3,750. This included rent of £500 for January 20X4.

(a) **Prepare the rental income account for the year ended 31 December 20X3 and close it off by showing the transfer to the statement of profit or loss.**

Rental income

Details	£	Details	£

The bank summary for the year shows payments for heat and light of £4,670. In February 20X4, an invoice for £1,290 was received in respect of the quarter ended 31 January 20X4.

BPP LEARNING MEDIA

(b) **Prepare the heat and light account for the year ended 31 December 20X3 and close it off by showing the transfer to the statement of profit or loss. Include dates.**

Heat and light

Date	Details	£	Date	Details	£

Task 4

This task is about preparing a trial balance and reconciliations.

You are working on the accounts of a business with a year end of 31 December. You have five extracts from the ledger accounts as at 31 December 20X3. You need to start preparing the trial balance as at 31 December 20X3.

(a) **Using all the information given below and the figures given in the table, enter amounts in the appropriate trial balance columns for the accounts shown.**

Do NOT enter zeros in unused column cells.

Do NOT enter any figures as negatives.

Bank

		£			£
31/12/X3	Balance b/f	5,635			

Sundry income

		£			£
			31/12/X3	Balance b/f	1,050

This balance has been adjusted for prepaid income of £125 as at 31/12/X3.

Administration costs

		£			£
31/12/X3	Balance b/f	6,940			

This balance has been adjusted for prepaid expenses of £720 as at 31/12/X3.

VAT

		£			£
			31/03/X7	Balance b/f	4,473

Extract from trial balance as at 31 December 20X3

Account	£	Debit £	Credit £
Accrued expenses			
Accrued income			
Capital	7,300		
Sales returns	456		
Bank			
Sundry income			
Administration costs			
VAT			
Prepaid expenses			
Prepaid income			

(b) **Use the following information to complete the table below to show the THREE adjustments you need to make to the cash book.**

The bank statement has been compared with the cash book and the following differences identified:

1. Bank charges of £121 were not entered in the cash book.

2. A cheque received from a customer for £280 has been recorded in the cash receipts book but it has been dishonoured and this has not yet been entered in the records.

3. A cheque for £765 to a supplier has not yet been presented for payment at the bank.

4. A direct debit of £650 to the local council appears only on the bank statement.

The balance showing on the bank statement is a debit of £660 and the balance in the cash book is a credit of £374.

BPP LEARNING MEDIA

Use the following table to show the THREE adjustments you need to make to the cash book.

Adjustment	Amount £	Debit ✓	Credit ✓

Task 5

This task is about recording adjustments in the extended trial balance and closing off accounts.

You are working on the final accounts of a business with a year end of 31 December 20X3. A trial balance has been drawn up and a suspense account opened with a debit balance of £1,772. You now need to make some corrections and adjustments for the year ended 31 December 20X3.

(a) **Record the adjustments needed on the extract from the extended trial balance to deal with the items below.**

You will not need to enter adjustments on every line. Do NOT enter zeros into unused cells.

(i) An allowance for doubtful debts of £2,420 is required at the year end.

(ii) A total column of £1,560 in the purchases returns day book was credited to the purchases ledger control account. All the other entries were made correctly.

(iii) Closing inventory for the year end 31 December 20X3 has not yet been recorded. Its value at cost is £12,860. Included in this figure are some items costing £1,250 that will be sold for £1,140.

(iv) A contra for £674 was debited to both the sales ledger control account and the purchases ledger control account.

Extract from extended trial balance

	Ledger balances		Adjustments	
	Debit £	Credit £	Debit £	Credit £
Allowance for doubtful debts adjustment				
Allowance for doubtful debts		2,563		
Closing inventory – SFP				
Closing inventory – SPL				
Bank overdraft		265		
Irrecoverable debts				
Purchases	567,239			
Purchases returns		8,922		
Purchases ledger control account		81,272		
Sales		926,573		
Sales returns	4,982			
Sales ledger control account	109,282			
Suspense	1,772			

(b) **The ledgers are ready to be closed off for the year ended 31 December 20X3. Show the correct entries to close off the sales returns account and insert an appropriate narrative.**

Account	Debit ✓	Credit ✓

BPP LEARNING MEDIA

Task 6

This task is about completing an extended trial balance and showing your accounting knowledge.

You have the following extended trial balance. The adjustments have already been correctly entered.

(a) **Extend the figures into the statement of profit or loss and statement of financial position columns.**

Do NOT enter zeros into unused column cells.

Make the columns balance by entering figures and a label in the correct places.

Extended trial balance

Ledger account	Ledger balances		Adjustments		Statement of profit or loss		Statement of financial position	
	£	£	£	£	£	£	£	£
Bank	7,281							
Capital		152,600						
Closing inventory			15,729	15,729				
Depreciation charge			27,600					
Commission income		18,272		3,825				
Drawings	40,000							
Accrued income			3,825					
Prepaid expenses			1,427					
Motor vehicles accumulated depreciation		88,900		27,600				
Motor vehicles at cost	170,000		4,300					
General expenses	67,298			1,427				
Opening inventory	17,268							
Purchases	98,245			726				
Purchases ledger control account		14,681	710					
Salaries	69,256							
Sales		201,675						
Sales ledger control account	17,504			710				
Suspense	3,574		726	4,300				
VAT		14,298						
	490,426	490,426	54,317	54,317				

(b) **When the cash book operates only as a book of prime entry there is a ledger account for Bank in the general ledger to which total receipts and payments are posted.**

✓	
	True
	False

BPP LEARNING MEDIA

BPP PRACTICE ASSESSMENT 3
ACCOUNTS PREPARATION

ANSWERS

Task 1

(a) – (c)

Non-current assets register

Description	Acquisition date	Cost £	Depreciation charges £	Carrying amount £	Funding method	Disposal proceeds £	Disposal date
Computer equipment							
COM265							
Year end 31/12/X1	1/1/X1	5,600.00	1,680.00	3,920.00	Credit		
Year end 31/12/X2			1,176.00	2,744.00			
Year end 31/12/X3			0.00	0.00		850.00	1/1/X3
COM399					Credit		
Year end 31/12/X2	1/1/X2	7,200.00	2,160.00	5,040.00			
Year end 31/12/X3			**1,512.00**	**3,528.00**			
Machinery							
MAC434							
Year end 31/12/X1	1/7/X1	12,940.00	3,235.00	9,705.00	Credit		
Year end 31/12/X2			3,235.00	6,470.00			
Year end 31/12/X3			**3,235.00**	**3,235.00**			
MAC637	1/5/X3	8,940.00			Credit		
Year end 31/12/X3			**2,235.00**	**6,705.00**			

Task 2

(a)

Machines at cost

	£		£
Balance b/d	12,500	Disposal account	4,000
Bank	1,000	Balance c/d	12,000
Part-exchange allowance	2,500		
	16,000		16,000

Machines accumulated depreciation

	£		£
Disposals account	1,440	Balance b/d	4,500
Balance c/d	3,060		
	4,500		4,500

Disposal account

	£		£
Machines at cost	4,000	Part exchange allowance	2,500
		Machines accumulated depreciation	1,440
		Statement of profit or loss	60
	4,000		4,000

(b)

✓	
	Cash purchase
✓	Hire purchase
	Borrowing
	Part exchange

Task 3

(a) Rental income

Details	£	Details	£
Balance b/d	1,000	Bank	3,750
Balance c/d	500		
Statement of profit or loss	2,250		
	3,750		3,750

(b) Heat and light

Date	Details	£	Date	Details	£
31/12	Balance c/d	860	1/1	Balance b/d	345
31/12	Bank	4,670	31/12	Statement of profit or loss	5,185
		5,530			5,530

Task 4

(a) Extract from trial balance as at 31 December 20X3

Account	£	Debit £	Credit £
Accrued expenses			
Accrued income			
Capital	7,300		7,300
Sales returns	456	456	
Bank		5,635	
Sundry income			1,050
Administration costs		6,940	
VAT			4,473
Prepaid expenses		720	
Prepaid income			125

(b)

Adjustment	Amount £	Debit ✓	Credit ✓
Adjustment for 1	121		✓
Adjustment for 2	280		✓
Adjustment for 4	650		✓

Task 5

(a) Extract from extended trial balance

	Ledger balances		Adjustments	
	Debit £	Credit £	Debit £	Credit £
Allowance for doubtful debts adjustment				143
Allowance for doubtful debts		2,563	143	
Closing inventory – SFP			12,750	
Closing inventory – SFP				12,750
Bank overdraft		265		
Irrecoverable debts				
Purchases	567,239			
Purchases returns		8,922		
Purchases ledger control account		81,272	3,120	
Sales		926,573		
Sales returns	4,982			
Sales ledger control account	109,282			1,348
Suspense	1,772		1,348	3,120

BPP
LEARNING MEDIA

(b)

Account	Debit ✓	Credit ✓
Statement of profit or loss	✓	
Sales returns		✓
Transfer of sales returns for year ended 31 December 20X3 to statement of profit or loss		

Task 6

(a) Extended trial balance

Ledger account	Ledger balances		Adjustments		Statement of profit or loss		Statement of financial position	
	£	£	£	£	£	£	£	£
Bank	7,281						7,281	
Capital		152,600						152,600
Closing inventory			15,729	15,729		15,729	15,729	
Depreciation charge			27,600		27,600			
Commission income		18,272		3,825		22,097		
Drawings	40,000						40,000	
Accrued income			3,825				3,825	
Prepaid expenses			1,427				1,427	
Motor vehicles accumulated depreciation		88,900		27,600				116,500
Motor vehicles at cost	170,000		4,300				174,300	
General expenses	67,298			1,427	65,871			
Opening inventory	17,268				17,268			
Purchases	98,245			726	97,519			
Purchases ledger control account		14,681	710					13,971
Salaries	69,256				69,256			
Sales		201,675				201,675		
Sales ledger control account	17,504			710			16,794	
Suspense	3,574		726	4,300				
VAT		14,298						14,298
Net loss						38,013	38,013	
	490,426	490,426	54,317	54,317	277,514	277,514	297,369	297,369

(b)

✓	
✓	True
	False

BPP
LEARNING MEDIA

BPP PRACTICE ASSESSMENT 4
ACCOUNTS PREPARATION

Time allowed: 2 hours

Task 1

This task is about recording information for non-current assets for a business known as Markham Ltd. The business is registered for VAT and its year end is 30 June.

The following is a purchase invoice received by Markham Ltd:

Office Solutions Ltd Unit 7 Tenton Industrial Estate TN14 5YJ	Invoice 9746	Date:	1 March 20X3
To:	Markham Ltd 14 The Green Tenton TN3 4ZX		
Description	Item number	Quantity	£
Corner office suite	OF477	1	1,950.00
Delivery and assembly charges		1	150.00
Printer ink cartridges		20	160.00
Net			2,260.00
VAT @ 20%			452.00
Total			2,712.00
Settlement terms: strictly 30 days net.			

The following information relates to the sale of an item of factory machinery:

Identification number	MN864
Date of sale	1 January 20X3
Selling price excluding VAT	£1,050.00

- Markham Ltd's policy is to recognise items of capital expenditure over £500 as non-current assets.

- Office equipment and furniture is depreciated at 20% per annum using the straight line method. There are no residual values.

- Factory machinery is depreciated at 25% per annum using the diminishing balance method.

- A full year's depreciation is charged in the year of acquisition and none in the year of sale.

Record the following information in the non-current assets register below:

(a) Any acquisitions of non-current assets during the year ended 30 June 20X3
(b) Any disposals of non-current assets during the year ended 30 June 20X3
(c) Depreciation for the year ended 30 June 20X3

Non-current assets register

Description	Acquisition date	Cost £	Depreciation charges £	Carrying amount £	Funding method	Disposal proceeds £	Disposal date
Factory machinery							
MN864	01/02/X1	15,600.00					
Year end 30/06/X1			3,900.00	11,700.00	Credit		
Year end 30/06/X2			2,925.00	8,775.00			
Year end 30/06/X3							
MN982	01/01/X2	9,400.00			Credit		
Year end 30/06/X2			2,350.00	7,050.00			
Year end 30/06/X3							
Office equipment							
OF025	01/04/X1	12,940.00					
Year end 30/06/X1			2,588.00	10,352.00	Credit		
Year end 30/06/X2			2,588.00	7,764.00			
Year end 30/06/X3							
Year end 30/06/X3							

BPP LEARNING MEDIA

Task 2

This task is about recording non-current asset information in the general ledger and other non-current asset matters.

- You are working on the accounts of a business that is registered for VAT. The business's year end is 31 December 20XX.
- On 1 September 20XX the business bought a new motor vehicle costing £15,000 excluding VAT.
- The vehicle's residual value is expected to be £3,000 excluding VAT.
- The business's depreciation policy for motor vehicles is 20% per annum on a straight line basis. A full year's depreciation is charged in the year of acquisition and none in the year of disposal.
- Depreciation has already been entered into the accounts for the business's existing motor vehicles.

Make entries to account for:

(a) **The purchase of the new motor vehicle**
(b) **The depreciation on the new motor vehicle**

On each account, show clearly the balance carried down or transferred to the statement of profit or loss.

Motor vehicles at cost

	£		£
Balance b/d	35,000		

Motor vehicles accumulated depreciation

	£		£
		Balance b/d	9,400

Depreciation charge

	£		£
Balance b/d	6,300		

(c) When non-current assets are depreciated using the straight line method, an equal amount is charged for each year of the asset's life.

✓	
	True
	False

Task 3

This task is about accounting for accruals and prepayments and preparing a trial balance.

You are working on the final accounts of a business for the year ended 31 December 20X3. In this task, you can ignore VAT.

You have the following information:

Balances as at:	1 January 20X3
	£
Accrual of rental income	2,100
Accrual of selling expenses	1,445

The bank summary for the year shows receipts of rental income of £4,850. This included rent of £600 for January 20X4.

(a) **Prepare the rental income account for the year ended 31 December 20X3 and close it off by showing the transfer to the statement of profit or loss.**

Rental income

Details	£	Details	£

The bank summary for the year shows payments for selling expenses of £5,770. In February 20X4, an invoice for £2,385 was received in respect of the quarter ended 31 January 20X4.

BPP LEARNING MEDIA

(b) **Prepare the selling expenses account for the year ended 31 December 20X3 and close it off by showing the transfer to the statement of profit or loss. Include dates.**

Selling expenses

Date	Details	£	Date	Details	£

Task 4

This task is about preparing a trial balance and reconciliations.

You are working on the accounts of a business with a year end of 31 December. You have five extracts from the ledger accounts as at 31 December 20X3. You need to start preparing the trial balance as at 31 December 20X3.

(a) **Using all the information given below and the figures given in the table, enter amounts in the appropriate trial balance columns for the accounts shown.**

   Do NOT enter zeros in unused column cells.

   Do NOT enter any figures as negatives.

Allowance for doubtful debts adjustment

		£			£
31/12/X3	Balance b/f	660			

Disposal of non-current asset

		£			£
			31/12/X3	Balance b/f	1,200

Office costs

		£			£
31/12/X3	Balance b/f	2,950			

Included in this balance is an amount for accrued expenses of £570 as at 31/12/X3.

Recycling rebates

		£			£
			31/12/X3	Balance b/f	3,560

Included in this balance is an amount for accrued income of £250 as at 31/12/X3.

VAT

		£			£
			31/12/X3	Balance b/f	1,222

Extract from trial balance as at 31 December 20X3

Account	£	Debit £	Credit £
Accrued expenses			
Accrued income			
Purchases returns	8,400		
Discounts allowed	1,556		
Discounts received	2,027		
Allowance for doubtful debts adjustment			
Disposal of non-current asset			
Office costs			
Recycling rebates			
VAT			
Prepaid expenses			
Prepaid income			

(b) **Use the following information to complete the table below to show the THREE adjustments you need to make to the cash book.**

The bank statement has been compared with the cash book and the following differences identified:

1. A standing order of £269 has not been entered in the cash book.

2. A cheque received from a customer for £500 has been recorded in the cash receipts book but the bank has informed us that the cheque was subsequently dishonoured.

3. A cheque for £940 to a supplier has not yet been presented for payment at the bank.

4. A direct debit of £485 to an utility company appears only on the bank statement.

The balance showing on the bank statement is a debit of £890 and the balance in the cash book is a credit of £576.

Use the following table to show the THREE adjustments you need to make to the cash book.

Adjustment	Amount £	Debit ✓	Credit ✓

. . . .

Task 5

This task is about recording adjustments in the extended trial balance and closing off accounts.

You are the accountant preparing the final accounts of a business with a year end of 31 December 20X5. A trial balance has been drawn up and a suspense account opened with a debit balance of £2,098. You now need to make some corrections and adjustments for the year ended 31 December 20X5.

(a) **Record the adjustments needed on the extract from the extended trial balance to deal with the items below.**

You will not need to enter adjustments on every line. Do NOT enter zeros into unused cells.

(i) An allowance for doubtful debts of £3,200 is required at the year end.

(ii) A total column of £1,885 in the purchases returns day book was credited to the purchases ledger control account. All the other entries were made correctly.

(iii) Closing inventory for the year end 31 December 20X5 has not yet been recorded. Its value at cost is £13,185. Included in this figure are some items costing £1,575 that will be sold for £1,400.

(iv) A contra for £836 was debited to both the sales ledger control account and the purchases ledger control account.

Extract from extended trial balance

	Ledger balances		Adjustments	
	Debit £	Credit £	Debit £	Credit £
Allowance for doubtful debts adjustment				
Allowance for doubtful debts		2,888		
Closing inventory – SFP				
Closing inventory – SPL				
Bank overdraft		590		
Irrecoverable debts				
Purchases	675,564			
Purchases returns		9,247		
Purchases ledger control account		92,597		
Sales		843,898		
Sales returns	5,307			
Sales ledger control account	98,607			
Suspense	2,098			

(b) **The ledgers are ready to be closed off for the year ended 31 December 20X5. Show the correct entries to close off the purchases returns account and insert an appropriate narrative.**

Account	Debit ✓	Credit ✓

BPP LEARNING MEDIA

Task 6

This task is about completing an extended trial balance and showing your accounting knowledge.

You have the following extended trial balance. The adjustments have already been correctly entered.

(a) **Extend the figures into the statement of profit or loss and statement of financial position columns.**

Do NOT enter zeros into unused column cells.

Make the columns balance by entering figures and a label in the correct places.

Extended trial balance

Ledger account	Ledger balances £	Ledger balances £	Adjustments £	Adjustments £	Statement of profit or loss £	Statement of profit or loss £	Statement of financial position £	Statement of financial position £
Machinery at cost	200,000		3,400					
Machinery accumulated depreciation		125,000		14,600				
Closing inventory			9,433	9,433				
Sales ledger control account	25,775			399				
Accrued income			249					
Prepaid expenses			765					
Bank	7,281							
Capital		150,000						
Drawings	10,000							
Purchases ledger control account		17,493	399					
VAT		8,965						
Sales		195,433						
Opening inventory	13,254							
Purchases	128,994			2,458				
Commission income		7,893		249				
Salaries	75,606							
General expenses	42,932			765				
Depreciation charge			14,600					
Suspense	942		2,458	3,400				
	504,784	504,784	31,304	31,304				

(b) **A debit balance on the cash book means that the business has funds available.**

✓	
	True
	False

BPP
LEARNING MEDIA

BPP PRACTICE ASSESSMENT 4
ACCOUNTS PREPARATION

ANSWERS

Task 1

(a) – (c)

Non-current assets register

Description	Acquisition date	Cost £	Depreciation charges £	Carrying amount £	Funding method	Disposal proceeds £	Disposal date
Factory machinery							
MN864	01/02/X1	15,600.00					
Year end 30/06/X1			3,900.00	11,700.00	Credit		
Year end 30/06/X2			2,925.00	8,775.00			
Year end 30/06/X3			0.00	0.00		1,050.00	01/01/X3
MN982	01/01/X2	9,400.00			Credit		
Year end 30/06/X2			2,350.00	7,050.00			
Year end 30/06/X3			**1,762.50**	**5,287.50**			
Office equipment							
OF025	01/04/X1	12,940.00					
Year end 30/06/X1			2,588.00	10,352.00	Credit		
Year end 30/06/X2			2,588.00	7,764.00			
Year end 30/06/X3			**2,588.00**	**5,176.00**			
OF477	01/03/X3	2,100.00			Credit		
Year end 30/06/X3			**420.00**	**1,680.00**			

Task 2

(a) and (b)

Motor vehicles at cost

	£		£
Balance b/d	35,000	**Balance c/d**	**50,000**
Purchases ledger control	**15,000**		
	50,000		50,000

Motor vehicles accumulated depreciation

	£		£
Balance c/d	11,800	Balance b/d	9,400
		Depreciation charge	2,400
	11,800		11,800

Depreciation charge

	£		£
Balance b/d	6,300	Statement of profit or loss	8,700
Motor vehicles accumulated depreciation	2,400		
	8,700		8,700

(c)

✓	
✓	True
	False

:::

Task 3

(a) **Rental income**

Details	£	Details	£
Balance b/d	2,100	Bank	4,850
Balance c/d	600		
Statement of profit or loss	2,150		
	4,850		4,850

BPP
LEARNING MEDIA

(b) Selling expenses

Date	Details	£	Date	Details	£
31/12	Bank	5,770	1/1	Balance b/d	1,445
31/12	Balance c/d	1,590	31/12	Statement of profit or loss	5,915
		7,360			7,360

Task 4

(a) Extract from trial balance as at 31 December 20X3

Account	£	Debit £	Credit £
Accrued expenses			570
Accrued income		250	
Purchases returns	8,400		8,400
Discounts allowed	1,556	1,556	
Discounts received	2,027		2,027
Allowance for doubtful debts adjustment		660	
Disposal of non-current asset			1,200
Office costs		2,950	
Recycling rebates			3,560
VAT			1,222
Prepaid expenses			
Prepaid income			

(b)

Adjustment	Amount £	Debit ✓	Credit ✓
Adjustment for 1	269		✓
Adjustment for 2	500		✓
Adjustment for 4	485		✓

Task 5

(a) Extract from extended trial balance

	Ledger balances		Adjustments	
	Debit £	Credit £	Debit £	Credit £
Allowance for doubtful debts adjustment			312	
Allowance for doubtful debts		2,888		312
Closing inventory – SFP			13,010	
Closing inventory – SPL				13,010
Bank overdraft		590		
Irrecoverable debts				
Purchases	675,564			
Purchases returns		9,247		
Purchases ledger control account		92,597	3,770	
Sales		843,898		
Sales returns	5,307			
Sales ledger control account	98,607			1,672
Suspense	2,098		1,672	3,770

BPP
LEARNING MEDIA

(b)

Account	Debit ✓	Credit ✓
Purchases returns	✓	
Statement of profit or loss		✓
Transfer of purchases returns for year ended 31 December 20X5 to statement of profit or loss		

Task 6

(a) Extended trial balance

Ledger account	Ledger balances		Adjustments		Statement of profit or loss		Statement of financial position	
	£	£	£	£	£	£	£	£
Machinery at cost	200,000		3,400				203,400	
Machinery accumulated depreciation		125,000		14,600				139,600
Closing inventory			9,433	9,433		9,433	9,433	
Sales ledger control account	25,775			399			25,376	
Accrued income			249				249	
Prepaid expenses			765				765	
Bank	7,281						7,281	
Capital		150,000						150,000
Drawings	10,000						10,000	
Purchases ledger control account		17,493	399					17,094
VAT		8,965						8,965
Sales		195,433				195,433		
Opening inventory	13,254				13,254			
Purchases	128,994			2,458	126,536			
Commission income		7,893		249		8,142		
Salaries	75,606				75,606			
General expenses	42,932			765	42,167			
Depreciation charge			14,600		14,600			
Suspense	942		2,458	3,400				
Net loss						59,155	59,155	
	504,784	504,784	31,304	31,304	272,163	272,163	315,659	315,659

(b)

✓	
✓	True
	False

BPP LEARNING MEDIA